MULTICULTURAL EDUCATION IN PRACTICE:

Transforming One Community at a Time

Olivia M. Gallardo & Lettie Ramirez

In Honor of Dr. Alma Flor Ada

Published by: VELÁZQUEZ PRESS,
A Division of Academic Learning Company, LLC

CABE:
16033 E. San Bernardino Rd.
Covina, CA 91722-3900
www.bilingualeducation.org

Velázquez Press:
9682 Telstar Ave. Ste 110
El Monte, CA 91731 USA
Visit www.VelazquezPress.com

Follow us on Facebook visit Facebook.com/MulticulturalEducation

ISBN 10: 1-59495-068-7
ISBN 13: 978-1-59495-068-1

Printed in the United States of America

First Edition
17 16 15 14 13 12   1 2 3 4 5

Library of Congress Control Number: 2012932972

MULTICULTURAL EDUCATION IN PRACTICE: TRANSFORMING ONE COMMUNITY AT A TIME

Part One

Breaking Down the Barriers of Institutional Racism

Poem xxvii
   Sometimes Beautiful
   Christopher Knaus

Chapter 1 1
   Going Beyond Heroes and Holidays:
   Scaffolding Multicultural Practices
   Lettie Ramírez and Olivia M. Gallardo

Chapter 2 13
   Transforming Pancho Villa
   Sergio Perez

Chapter 3 25
   Unlearning Racism:
   A Teacher's Journey Leads to School Transformation
   Patricia Perez

Chapter 4 35
   Collaboration and Community Transformation Center Stage:
   When Teachers, Youth and Parents Actively Value Difference
   Rose Borunda and Gwyn Bruch

Chapter 5 51
   Honoring and Sustaining Heritage Languages:
   Strategies for the Non-Bilingual Teacher
   Zaida Mccall-Perez

Part Two

Promoting Change by Empowering Parents

Poem
  Round Them Up and Send Them Back
  Susana Hernandez

Chapter 6 65
  Transformative Education in Action Through the One Mind Group:
  How Recently Immigrated, Korean-American Parents of
  Children with Special Needs Become Active Parent Advocates
  Eun Mi Cho

Chapter 7 81
  Empowered Parents Transform School Districts:
  Fighting for Bilingual Programs
  Olivia Gallardo

Part Three

Transformative Higher Education: Learning by Example

Poem 95
  By Myself
  Stephen Fisher

Chapter 8 97
  Teacher Education Students Share Their Voices:
  The Exponential Effect of Transformation
  Evangelina "Gigi" Brignoni

Chapter 9 115
  Preparing Pre-Service Spanish Bilingual Teachers to Develop a Vision for
  Transformative Education
  Josephine Arce

Part Four

Transformative Education: Empowerment and Leadership

Poem
    Slammin the System
    Andre Brunetti

Chapter 10 129
    Teaching for Voice:
    Instructional Strategies for Empowering Youth
        Chris Knaus

Chapter 11 157
    The Role of Inquiry in Teacher Leadership:
    Examining Student Achievement in Multicultural Settings
        Barbara A. Storms and Gloria M. Rodriguez

Chapter 12 169
    Teaching Through the Arts:
    A Missing Link in Bilingual and Multicultural Education
        Peter Baird

FORWARD

Multicultural Education in Practice: Transforming One Community at a Time presents a compelling challenge to the prevailing paradigm of American education and how student achievement is conceptualized. The experiences reflected in the text challenge us to speak the truth when we raise issues of race, class, and gender. Similarly, and just as intensely, we are energized and our faith in our abilities to transform education collaboratively is reinforced.

For too long, children of diverse linguistic and cultural backgrounds have been victims of educational systems that foster institutional racism and neglect. Indeed, and more to the point, such systems should be viewed as *violent* institutions because they perpetuate a sense of helplessness and hopelessness. My own work on school violence, gangs, drug abuse, teen pregnancy, and low academic achievement underscores the tendency to treat such critical issues as separate and distinct problems in need of clinical solutions from educational experts. Rather, we must view such challenges as collective symptoms of an underlying educational cancer, resulting from a loss of faith in our schools and those who lead them. Children and their families suffer in silence.

Paulo Freire (1997) noted, *"Hopelessness and despair are both the consequence and the cause of inaction and immobilism"* (p. 9). In *Multicultural Education in Practice,* the writers give us real hope through their experiences and engagement with children, parents, and the community. The writers disagree vigorously, eloquently, and persuasively with the existing educational status quo and present us instead with numerous examples of what true transformative education and leadership can mean. Clearly, through their work, Multicultural Education becomes an operational concept. Moreover, their work underscores the intense struggle necessary to conceptualize and implement an empowering pedagogy that genuinely affirms and deeply respects the wisdom that children and their parents bring to the transformative process.

There is an old saying in the Latino community--children are truly the only ones who tell the truth. Children do not have the inclination, indeed the burden, of speaking *in code* as adults sometimes do. The wisdom inherent in this adage speaks to all educators and reflects the beautiful simplicity with which children of all cultures view life and their use of language. If we are willing to truly listen, children can renew and re-energize our sense of purpose, urgency and responsibility in shaping effective and responsive educational systems. Indeed, they and their parents can be our teachers.

The writers of *Multicultural Education in Practice* challenge all educators to speak the truth from the *corazòn* and commit themselves to real action and reflection in their own work. The themes highlighting an inclusive and innovative classroom curriculum, and school-wide re-culturing, form the core of what ultimately leads to political transformation. The courageous authors of this text are not only focused on academic achievement, but also on educational relevance, justice, and equity.

Francisco Reveles, Ed.D.
Professor and Chair
Educational Leadership & Policy Studies Department
California State University, Sacramento

ACKNOWLEDGEMENTS

We are grateful to our colleagues, mentors, and students at California State University, East Bay, California State University, Sacramento, University of San Francisco, and University of Texas, El Paso. Our work in these institutions has helped us meet and work closely with dedicated and talented educators who have guided our professional development and who have pushed us to face new challenges that have helped us to grow personally and professionally.

In addition, we are thankful to educators with whom we have worked in schools and universities across the USA and other parts of the world: in particular the Hayward Unified School District, Oakland Unified School District, Universidad Autonoma de Guadalajara, and Ysleta Independent School District.

We would like to thank our colleagues who have contributed to this book. This book was possible because of their hard work and their willingness to share their research with us. Their passion and dedication have also transformed our lives.

We are grateful to Diane Farrer, Santa McGill and Dorine Mendelsohn for their editing skills, and especially to Mary Bobik our "special" editor, as well as to our families. A special thank you to Eriberto Gallardo who always helps us when we are looking for that specific word. It is our hope that the words and actions of these authors will make a difference in schools and communities all over the world.

Lettie and Olivia

DEDICATION

Dearest Alma Flor,

Yes, dearest Dr. Alma Flor Ada . . . ever present in our hearts and minds. We lovingly dedicate this book to you, a small reflection of how you have taught us to build a better world, and shown us how to heal, thought by thought, action by action, and silence by silence. This book is an expression of the road you continue to write, a road not easily travelled, but a road with infinite possibilities, a more sane and healthy way of living together, caring for one another and our planet. Some of us have been lucky enough to be your lifelong students, friends and allies, and others by association with the words that you speak, and the speaking that you write, all a representation of the work that WE DO.

This dialectical of "the words that we write lead us to the words that we speak, and the work that WE DO leads us to a reflection of words that we speak and write", is encapsulated in the chapters of this book. The writing here reveals the practice of transformative education. It lays bare the difficult, convoluted and often dissonant conundrum that is inherent to the inspection of inequitable social and ecological structures. These writings also represent the glow of responsibility, the willingness not to accept what is, but to work towards what can be. There are limitations, and much to be contemplated in these writings; extensions and changes of direction still need to be taken by the writers, yet this is all part of the transformational process.

As you have taught us so well, we are never all at the same place in our thoughts and understandings, but through our own internal rage, patience, diligence, pain and dialogue, each layered with a critical construction of "listening loudly," these writings affirm the belief that we all have something to offer and knowledge to share. They demonstrate once again that we can come to understand and learn collectively from one another, to move forward critically, with our thinking/writing/speaking out to action process.

How fortunate for us that you came into this world, that you were guided to stand firmly and resolutely on the shoulders of those who came before us, and are always with us, in solidarity, pain and the search for understanding. We are privileged to have you in our lives as you continue to model transformation and actively question the "hidden agendas" of educational and social institutions, and those who all too often harbor underlying messages of who is important and who is not, which languages and cultures are of value

and which are not, and those who are exclusionary in their focus on maintaining power so obtusely--all feigned and fogged for the purpose of coercive marginalization, however benignly presented. As demonstrated in these writings, your work shines forth as a guide to a personal as well as institutional conceptual framework for social and ecological justice.

You have taught us to fly, to dream, to problem-pose and to reach out to the world as an instigator for critical transformation and understanding. You embrace us so lovingly as we go about our daily work of helping others to see their self-worth and their ability to affect positive, thoughtful, and critical change. We hope you will find happiness and joy in these extensions of your own work, and rest in the knowledge that NONE of your efforts have been in vain. We will continue to encourage the voice of those coming after us, to ensure a critical pedagogy of questioning and action.

Thank you for being who you are, for the strength that you have given so freely, for the horizons you have opened to us. We are living through unquestionably disconcerting, aggressive and frightening times. You have also lived through challenging and difficult times and found ways to maintain positive values and a strong work ethic to continue the think, speak, write cycle of action and ally building. The ideas presented in this book are a tribute to the power of Transformative Education that you have bestowed on us, from your very heart and soul.

In greatest gratitude, as always . . .

Nancy Jean Smith
CSU Stanislaus
Stockton, California

ABOUT THE AUTHORS

Josephine Arce is an Associate professor at San Francisco State University. Her research focuses on literacy development for English Language Learners, bilingual students, two-way Spanish immersion, bilingual education and teacher education. Her theoretical constructs derive from critical theory, critical pedagogy, and bilingual education. She coordinates the Master of Arts: Concentration Language & Literacy, Department of Elementary Education.

Peter Baird is an Associate Professor in the Bilingual/Multicultural Education Department at CSU Sacramento, where he has taught since 2000. He also draws from 10 years of experience as a bilingual elementary classroom teacher in Sacramento and Galt, California, and earlier work experiences in journalism, music, civil rights activism, and in the printing industry. In May of 2001, he completed his dissertation under the guidance of Dr. Alma Flor Ada and received a doctorate in International and Multicultural Education from the University of San Francisco. He may be contacted at pbaird@csus.edu.

Rose Borunda received her doctorate in International and Multicultural Education from the University of San Francisco. She is the Chair of the Counseling Department and teaches graduate courses in the Department of Counselor Education at California State University, Sacramento. Her previous professional experiences include advocacy as the Executive Director of Child Assault Prevention, Inc., for Contra Costa County, a junior high school counselor in Pittsburg, California, and a high school counselor and leadership coordinator. She has received various awards for her work in furthering the cause for equity and social justice. Dr. Borunda's work with teachers and students has been recognized throughout California.

Evangelina "Gigi" Brignoni earned her doctorate from Claremont Graduate University in 2004. Currently, she is an assistant professor of ESL methodology, literacy, and Spanish language arts at the University of Nebraska at Omaha working with future teachers and graduate students. She has been a bilingual educator since 1978, working in the classroom, kindergarten through sixth grade, and assisting other teachers as a resource coordinator. In 1996, Dr. Brignoni became a Writing Fellow of the UCLA's

Writing Project. She served as a consultant for the Writing Reform Institute for Teachers of English (WRITE) and guided Los Angeles County upper grade teachers on how best to help English Learners write academically. Dr. Brignoni believes strongly that teachers will teach writing more effectively if they themselves write and, as writers, teachers will share their stories and, in turn, so will their students.

For the past 30 years, **Gwyneth Bruch** has been active in local theatre, an avocation that led to her becoming a high school drama teacher. For the past ten years she has taught English in a program for marginalized sophomores which she helped start. Her only son is now a junior at Western Washington University, working with Men Against Violence. He is her constant source of inspiration and strength. She recently retired from her position as a choreographer of the high school show choir to focus on issues of equity, diversity, and social justice, in addition to her work with drama and marginalized populations. She thanks her husband for his understanding and infinite patience in support of her work.

Eun Mi Cho is Assistant Professor at California State University, Sacramento in the Special Education Department. She is the founder and coordinator, of the "One Mind Group" in the Sacramento and San Jose area. This association brings together parents of English Learners with Disabilities. Her interest in working with Korean parents has created new opportunities for parents to improve the intercultural communication and collaboration between special education professionals and Asian American parents. She received her doctorate from the University of San Francisco in International and Multicultural Education focusing on second language acquisition and Special Education.

Olivia M. Gallardo received her doctorate from the University of San Francisco in International and Multicultural Education. She has 20 years of teaching experience in bilingual classrooms working with students from kindergarten to grade twelve. In the Department of Education at California State University East Bay, she has taught courses in second language learning, multicultural education, and children's literature. Dr. Gallardo's work with grants has led to the development of training and workshops that prepare teacher candidates for careers in science and math. She works as a consultant to districts throughout California in the area of parent educational leadership. Dr. Gallardo believes that bridging the home culture to the school culture provides children and parents the beginning needed for future leaders.

Christopher B. Knaus studies racism in education and focuses on resisting such racism through developing urban students' voices. He also uses Critical Race Theory to examine educational policy and frame ways of educating in culturally affirming, responsive, and relevant ways that decenter standards-based methods. Dr. Knaus earned his doctorate from the University of Washington, and his first book was *Race, Racism, and Multiraciality in American Education*. Currently, he teaches at California State University, East Bay.

Zaida McCall-Perez is an Associate Professor at Holy Names University in Oakland, where she coordinates the Masters of Education program and the Bilingual Authorization for Teachers. She was born in Puerto Rico and is bilingual. She earned her doctorate in International Multicultural Education from the University of San Francisco and her Masters in Special Education from San Francisco State University. As a consultant she assists schools in becoming more culturally and linguistically responsive to their communities, and in decreasing racial/ethnic disproportionality in Special Education. As a parent advocate, she assists Spanish-speaking parents to become more effective partners with their child's school. She coaches thesis and dissertation students throughout the U.S. and Puerto Rico.

Patricia Pérez received her doctorate from the University of San Francisco in Organizational Leadership. She has worked as a Grant Coordinator and Early Assessment Program Coordinator in the College of Education and Allied Studies at California State University, East Bay providing teachers direction and assistance in the classroom. She also works as a diversity consultant in a number of school districts in the San Francisco Bay Area. She holds an M.S. in Educational Leadership with an emphasis on urban teacher leadership, as well as an Administrative Services credential. Dr. Pérez has 10 years of teaching experience in bilingual classrooms at the elementary school level. Her interests focus on promoting educational excellence through equity in order to overcome institutional barriers that confront underserved students of diverse backgrounds.

Sergio O. Perez is an English teacher at Bel Air High School in El Paso, Texas. He currently holds a B.A. in English from California State University, Stanislaus and completed his Master's program in Educational Administration and Leadership at the University of Texas at El Paso. In 2004, he became a fellow as part of the West Texas Writing Project and is also the current sponsor of the literary club, which sponsors the publication of *The Chanter* literary magazine. His enthusiasm for social justice is rooted in his Multiculturalism studies, and he has worked closely with children who come from impoverished and non-English speaking backgrounds. Mr. Perez believes that the key to teaching successfully depends on valuing a child's identity.

Lettie Ramirez is a Professor in the College of Education and Allied Studies at California State University, East Bay. She is a strong advocate for teachers and English Language Learner students. Her focus of interest includes recruitment, retention, and professional development for teachers in addition to obtaining funding for these causes.
Dr. Ramirez currently is the director of Project SI: Sheltered Instruction and Project EBTI: East Bay Teacher Institute in addition to being the director of the CSU BCLAD International Program in Mexico.

Gloria M. Rodriguez is an Assistant Professor in the School of Education at the University of California at Davis. She holds a doctorate in Education in the Administration and Policy Analysis Program from Stanford University. Prior to earning her doctorate, Rodriguez worked in the public arena, conducting policy analysis at the local, county, and state levels, including a position with the California Legislative Analyst's Office. Dr. Rodriguez specializes in school finance, resource allocation, and educational leadership from a critical, social justice perspective. She also conducts work on the equity status of Latina/o students in the U.S. Her current research includes an investigation of "social justice leadership" to understand how educational leaders conceptualize and enact social justice commitments.

Barbara A. Storms received her doctorate from Northern Arizona University. She is a Professor at California State University, East Bay in the Department of Educational Leadership. Dr. Storms has been active in curriculum, instruction, and assessment reform efforts for twenty-five years, first as a secondary teacher and school administrator in urban schools, then as a program administrator/researcher at Educational Testing Service, and now as a faculty member at the university. Before joining CSUEB, Dr. Storms did extensive curriculum development work in language arts, literacy, and social studies in a large, urban school district in Southern California. Her particular curricular interest relates to writing instruction and the relationship between teacher training in writing instruction and student achievement. She helped to design and conduct the 1998 NAEP Special Study for Classroom Writing and has worked on state and national research and development projects related to content standards, performance assessment, and teacher induction.

POEMS

Andre Brunetti is a 6th grade teacher at West Contra Costa Unified. He is loved and respected by his students and colleagues for all the work he does to live and to teach what he believes. This poem was written at a time when Mr. Brunetti was just starting to teach, and the passage of time has not changed its strength.

Susana M. Hernandez received her M.A. from California State University at Los Angeles in Public Administration. Her work in the field of private foundations has exposed her to many of the prejudices that workers experience in private industry. Susana is the co-founder of Latin Inspired Designs. This company creates nutcrackers with an original Lation design. She continues to search for ways to enhance the richness of the Latino culture, and she feels that the history and tradition embedded in the Latino culture needs to be taught beyond the classroom.

Christopher Knaus is a professor at California State University, East Bay. He contributed a chapter to this book.

Stephen Fisher earned a degree in Early Childhood Education at the University of Nebraska at Omaha.

INTRODUCTION

Human beings are not built in silence, but in word,
in work, in action-reflection.

Paulo Freire

The culturally responsive classroom provides students with a curriculum that explores issues and themes relevant to their lives and their community. When inquiry becomes part of the culturally relevant school, identifying the problems or issues that lead to positive change becomes part of an ongoing process that develops an inclusive curriculum. This book provides the foundation for educators, counselors, teachers, and other practitioners to initiate the dialogue with their community in order to bring about the changes necessary for achieving equity and justice.

Part One

Breaking Down the Barriers of Institutional Racism includes three chapters that define what transformative education means and what it looks like when applied to actual practices in a school setting. Chapters 2, 3, and 4 demonstrate the positive impact our multi-ethnic communities, schools, and districts can achieve through collaborative means.

Chapter 1 introduces the four levels or approaches that characterize multicultural practices. A description of each level helps the reader to understand how equity and diversity require time and courageous commitment. The need for educating parents, teachers, principals, and other community members on the importance of valuing a culturally diverse society rarely goes beyond the classroom. This chapter introduces ideas that can lead to the transformation of a classroom, a school, and in other instances, a whole community. A brief description of each project follows with some questions at the end to begin the process of reflective reading and planning.

Chapter 2 "Transforming Pancho Villa" introduces us to the author, and from his description, the reader can identify with the changes many teachers go through as they try to do what is best for the students. Preparing the students for passing the test and learning English takes precedence over learning about the students and how best to work with them. The authors' transformation leads him to reflection and change in his attitudes as he recognizes the hegemonic practices existing in many schools.

In Chapter 3, "Unlearning Racism," the author describes how her inquisitiveness and education lead her on the path to change and school transformation. The result was the whole school working toward an equitable environment. The author begins by defining institutional racism and how its existence as an embedded practice separates children, teachers, and school personnel. The importance of this chapter is in its magnification of a problem that exists in schools, but most importantly when recognized, how it can be changed.

Chapter 4, on "Collaboration and Community Transformation Center Stage," delivers an impacting account of what is necessary for a high school to evolve into a truly equitable school society. From the macro to the micro levels, the transformation that must occur involves a critical examination of the process and procedures in place in a "traditional" classroom and the acceptance of these classroom structures. Readers experience the changes that are possible and how they can work toward positive interactions between different ethnic groups. The authors provide first-hand knowledge and practice that brought about unprecedented developments in a school drama program.

Chapter 5, on "Honoring and Sustaining Heritage Languages," shows that multicultural education values languages, and this chapter provides specific examples of how teaching can incorporate bilingualism into all classrooms. Specific strategies are provided for teachers who do not speak the heritage language.

Part Two

The two chapters in this section expand on the changes possible when parents and school leaders work together:

Chapter 6 on "Transformative Education in Action through The One Mind Group" gives an account of how a Korean community comes together and discovers how its empowerment provides the support that special education children need. Tradition, customs, and philosophy create strong Asian communities in America; however, they also create barriers. When provided with the opportunity to understand what special education means and what more needs to be done for their children, parents abandon the taboos from the past. The author, a member of the Korean community in the field of special education, understands the educational system, and through her leadership she has helped parents to learn how to advocate for their children.

Chapter 7 on "Empowered Parents Transform a School District" gives a historical account of one school districts' unwavering fight to save bilingual education. In a community with a significant number of Spanish speakers, identity, culture, and language provide constancy and security. This particular community found the students' education interrupted when the district did away with bilingual programs as a result of California voters' passage of Proposition 227. Parents felt that their children were victimized and the effects of Proposition 227 were harmful to their children's academic process. Transformation of the district came about when parents acted together to improve their children's education. Bilingual programs returned when a new District School Board was elected, with the support of these pro active parents and the community as a whole.

Part Three

This section demonstrates the power and significance of including historical and student *voice* in the curriculum. The authors' experiences highlight how critical theory revolutionizes the school curriculum. Students and teachers alike discover their voice when professors take the time to explore their own students' history and their own students' lives.

Chapter 8, "Teacher Education Students Share Their Voices," demonstrates the power of transformation when individuals come together and share their stories. The lessons teachers practice in the classroom prepare them better to understand the cultures they are exposed to through their students. The author believes that a well prepared teacher learns about the student's culture through classroom conversation and writing practice.

Chapter 9 on "Preparing Preservice Spanish, Bilingual Teachers to Develop a Vision for Transformative Education" presents educators with a model that integrates critical pedagogy strategies as part of the teaching practice to address the history of Latinos in the United States. This study engaged preservice bilingual credential candidates through a course content that promotes dialogues about Latinos' self and collective identity, socio-economic issues, power relations in educational settings, and society at large.

Part Four

Empowerment and Leadership continues the discussion on how student success is not always measured by tests and standards. Knowing the students' capabilities will take many paths, and each administrator, counselor, and educator can use his or her own background of experience and knowledge to help students succeed.

Chapter 10, the "Teaching for Voice," summarizes how transformative education successfully creates change and empowerment for the particular communities discussed in this book. It will elaborate on how the theoretical rationale underlying this theory creates a phenomenon traditional programs cannot match.

Chapter 11 on "The Role of Inquiry in Teacher Leadership" provides an in-depth discussion of the nature and place of collaborative inquiry in teacher leadership to foster greater academic achievement among diverse student populations. A definition of the explicit terms used in the chapter and establishment of a common language provide the reader with the understanding necessary to explore the potential impact of inquiry in multicultural settings.

Chapter 12, "Teaching through the Arts," reiterates the importance of praxis as an end and beginning to critical teaching. The author discusses the strength of critical theory and how it relates to the various studies detailed in the chapters of this book as well as his own. His transformative process mirrors that of many of the other authors who have made a difference in their schools and in their communities by following a journey that starts with one class and continues the rest of their lives.

Multicultural Education in Practice: Transforming One Community at a Time is an inquiry model that has led to needed changes in our schools. We are all at the crossroads--embarking on one journey or ending another. As educators and individuals with children as our main concern, we acknowledge that reflection and praxis never take place in a vacuum. It is not learned from one book, but it is practice, which leads each person to find transformation using critical inquiry.

Sometimes Beautiful
by Christopher Knaus
December 2008

We live in a terrible world
And sometimes, we're really beautiful

We live in a terrible world
Where students are shot, beat down, and beat at home
Where students strive push grow only to be told college is not for you
Where students are punished for speaking their voice, their minds, their hearts
Where more students leave high school without diplomas then go on to college

We live in a terrible world
Where parents are reminded of when they were shot, beat down, and beat at home
Where parents are reminded of their own previous school failures
Where parents are continually told they do not raise our children well
despite working 2 or 3 or sometimes 4 jobs
Where parents are told they are simply Not Doing Enough

We live in a terrible world
Where educators are told to save us all
But first, make sure everyone passes this and that standard, this and that test
Which has little to do with dodging bullets, helping parents break drug addictions, or
Modeling pride in who we are, the languages we speak, the families we love at home

We live in a terrible world
Placing all of our burdens, our racism, our poverty, our ignorance
On our youth, our children, our students, on young men and women
Still struggling to figure out how crazy this world really is
Placing all of our burdens, our racism, our poverty, our ignorance
On our educators, our teachers still struggling to figure out
How crazy this world really is

And in this terrible world
We have no choice but to be beautiful
To sing song our voices in multiple languages
To remind our students our educators our families our communities
That we are beautiful because
We express our voices magnificently
And if you're still listening to me
If you're still reading these words
Reflect on why you aren't taking notes
Get out your pen and write your mind
Because we are still learning still students
Still learning still students

And the one thing we know
Is that without your voice
This world will remain…Terrible.

Chapter 1

Going Beyond Heroes and Holidays:
Scaffolding Multicultural Practices

by Lettie Ramírez and Olivia M. Gallardo

*By accepting that all human beings have an avocation for learning and
that they are all constructors of knowledge; by seeing in themselves
and in others the capacity to name the world in order to transform it;
by refusing to be dominated by fear and assuming the risk and the glory
of truth; by all of that will we become truly educators and embrace our
destiny as protagonists of the extraordinary human adventure.*

Alma Flor Ada
(1995)

Introduction

Almost half a century has transpired since the Civil Rights movement began
with the courageous effort to move this country toward cultural plurality and respect for
the individual. In the field of multicultural education, these last fifty years have seen a
dramatic change in how we address diversity and equity. This is very important when
there are over 13 million students living in poverty and in K-12 grades (Children's
Defense Fund, 2005). Research in the past decade has concentrated on raising the bar
to meet the academic standards with slight attention paid to research using culturally
relevant pedagogy and the benefits that educators may gain using models that meet
both the academic and social needs of our students (Gay, 2000; Howard, 2001; Ladson-
Billings, 1994; Ramirez and Gallardo, 2001). Furthermore, many in the field of
education, and specifically educators working in settings with an increasingly multiethnic
student population, continue searching for practical models that have relevance to the
teachers and students' social and cultural realities.

The naturally evolving educational focus creates a paradigm shift from the
individual to the community model. Notably, when we are in a group where we do not
feel included, we are far more likely to guard our resources, strengths, and weaknesses to
protect ourselves from others (Wlodkowski & Ginsberg, 1995). The opposite occurs as

demonstrated by educators committed to change (Nodding, 1988; Valenzuela, 1999). As Valenzuela points out, a precondition to caring about school necessitates that students be engaged in a caring relationship with an adult at school. This, in essence, is the heart of a transformative curriculum.

In an effort to help teachers and other educators deal explicitly with cultural diversity, the move to include multicultural education in the teacher preparation program has brought equity and diversity to the forefront; however, this change, from what Banks calls Level 1, the Contributions Approach, to a Level 4, described as a Social Action Approach, requires time and courageous commitment.

Banks (1979), in his seminal work, brought to light the inconsistency with which textbooks incorporate in-depth knowledge about ethnic cultures and their experiences into the curriculum and how mainstream-centric curriculum supports, reinforces, and justifies the existing social, economic, and political structure. With this four-pronged approach, Banks gave multicultural education the solid pedagogic framework which teachers recognized as essential--to place students at the center of their self-discovery as participating members of their schools and communities and contributing agents for positive change. Banks transformed multicultural education when he formulated his Approaches to Multicultural Curriculum Reform, Neaphytos Richardson (2001). See Table 1.1.

| Table 1.1 ||
Approaches to Multicultural Curriculum	
Level 1 **Contributions Approach** Discrete cultural elements such as: food, artifacts, clothing, holidays, maps, heroes, music, art, dance, posters, geography, or climate	**Level 2** **Additive Approach** Content, concepts, themes and perspectives including: history of the culture; history and current circumstances of the immigrants; precepts guiding the culture; use of literature of the culture to provide depth of understanding; bibliographies; and useful websites
Level 3 **Transformation Approach** Learners seek out individuals of other cultures (cultural informants) to enhance their learning. The voices of members of the community are heard, and issues relevant to the community are discussed. The curriculum seeks to include the multiple perspectives of and new understandings gained by students.	**Level 4** **Social Action Approach** Authentic, generative problem themes are agreed upon, and a problem posing methodology is used. Curriculum is co-constructed through reflection and dialogue, where the role of the teacher is co-learner, listener, and facilitator, not conveyor of knowledge. Heightened awareness developed in class enables students to take action and intervene for themselves.

Figure 1.1
Teacher Levels applied in Classrooms

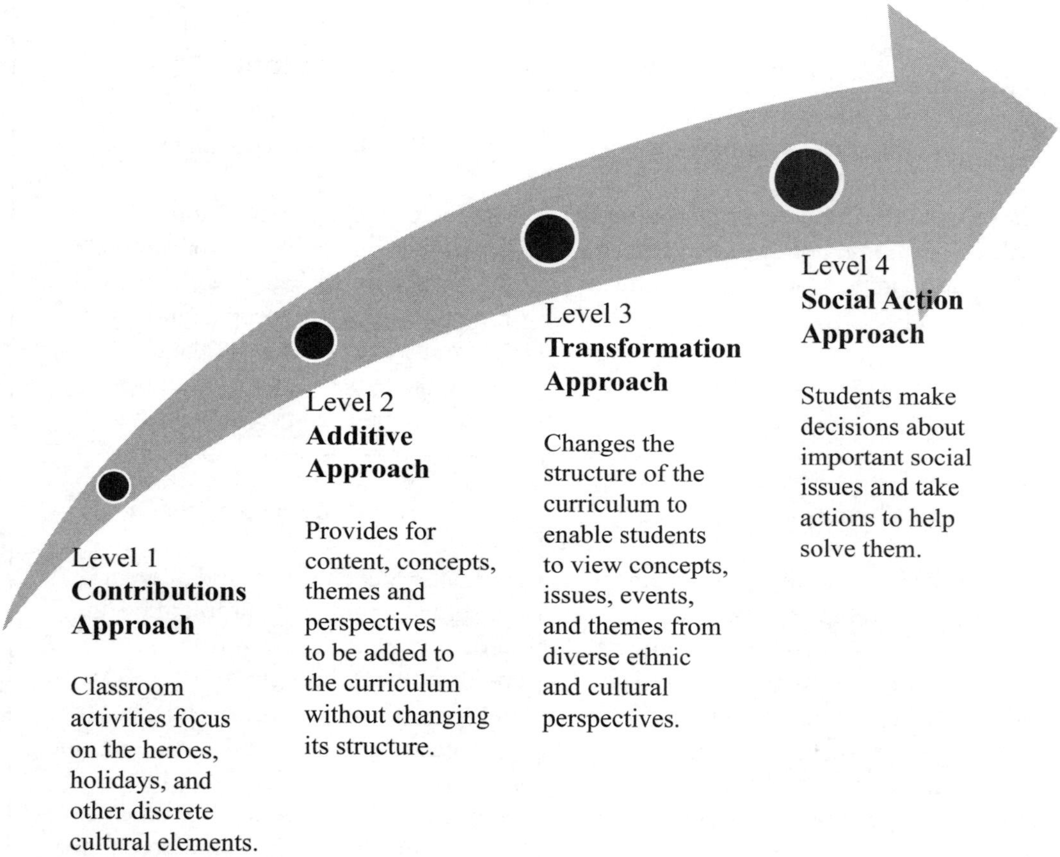

Level 1
Contributions
Approach

Classroom
activities focus
on the heroes,
holidays, and
other discrete
cultural elements.

Level 2
Additive
Approach

Provides for
content, concepts,
themes and
perspectives
to be added to
the curriculum
without changing
its structure.

Level 3
Transformation
Approach

Changes the
structure of the
curriculum to
enable students
to view concepts,
issues, events,
and themes from
diverse ethnic
and cultural
perspectives.

Level 4
Social Action
Approach

Students make
decisions about
important social
issues and take
actions to help
solve them.

Multicultural Education in Practice: Transforming One Community at a Time

This framework, (Figure 1.1), describes the levels teachers find themselves applying in the classroom. At the lowest level, the Contributions Approach, classroom activities focus on heroes, holidays, and distinct cultural elements. At the second level, the Additive Approach provides for content, concepts, themes, and perspectives to be added to the curriculum without changing its structure. Level three, the Transformation Approach, changes the structure of the curriculum to enable students to view concepts, issues, events, and themes from the perspective of diverse ethnic and cultural groups. At the fourth and highest level, the Social Action Approach, students make decisions on social issues important to their lives and take actions to help solve them.

Multicultural Education in Practice: Transforming One Community at a Time focuses on the third and fourth levels. When viewing school practices through a critical and multicultural lens, the educator aims to take the students beyond the traditional curriculum. Students become seekers of their own knowledge. The methodology guides the practice and the readings provide the models that reinforce change. Each of the authors, all practitioners in the field of education, shows how to scaffold successfully from Level 1 toward Level 4.

Beginning with Level 3, the transformative approach includes the multiple perspectives of teacher and student, leading to new understandings that emphasize content and process. Looking at Figure 1 Level 3, the goal of student empowerment begins by establishing a trust that affirms the importance of student voice. It states, *"The voices of all members of the community are heard, and issues relevant to the community are discussed. The curriculum seeks to include the multiple perspectives of and new understandings gained by students."* Level 3 tackles societal themes contributing to underachievement and the high dropout rate among all students, especially students of color. Nieto (1999) refers to the present state of our teaching as a mono-cultural education that reflects one reality, biased toward the dominant group. She argues, "What students learn represents only a fraction of what is available knowledge and those who decide what is most important make choices that are of necessity influenced by their own limited background, education and experience" (p.33). As noted, Level 3 is the "why" of multicultural education, and educators across the country are finding ways to modify the "one size fits all" traditional curriculum.

Level 4 becomes the juncture where the Theory of Social Knowledge develops, taking on the role of the builder. At this level, practitioners push up their sleeves and make the decision to find ways to bring about change. Mc Gee (1993) clarifies how, as constructors of knowledge, multicultural education brings about change following a rigorous program built on the theory of knowledge. As Nieto (1999) notes, multicultural education is not easy; if it were, everyone would be doing it. Teacher preparation institutions begin the process by providing teachers the theory. However, change requires more than providing the information; it requires bold steps, which Darder (1999) further elaborates on by explaining that the interaction of the theoretical perspective, the reflection of that practice, and the actions and decisions that follow are what make the difference between talking about multicultural theory and acting upon it.

Beginning the Process

Commitment and a search for knowledge involve various actions. Olson and Jaramillo (1999) in their development of a Theory of Action begin the process of change using a format that pushes for deeper thinking and clear articulation. Table 1.2 is included to assist practitioners new to this theory with a practical way to look at the problems they pose and help them in their search for outcomes. The Theory of Action is a sequence of linked actions and reactions that are in the minds of people when they go about any intervention or change process (Olson & Jaramillo 1999). See Table 1.2.

Table 1.2
Theory of Action

Problem Challenge	Activities	Result	Outcome
The problem is of concern	We think if we do...	It will result in these changes in how we go about doing things in school...	With this kind of student achievement outcome...
What is the problem?	What do you plan to do?	What changes can result from your planning?	Did you reach the desired outcomes?

Table 1.3
Theory of Social Knowledge

Change Needed	Reflection	Dialogue	Outcome
Posing the problem	How can we...	Feedback from participants	Each individual reaches a different place leading them back to posing another problem or challenge.

The Theory of Social Knowledge uses a similar introduction to pose a problem, and it uses a series of linked actions with the facilitator beginning the process. This theory, based on the foundations of critical pedagogy, employs Freire's principles of problem-posing to begin the process of self-empowerment through dialogue and reflection to develop *voice* or to explore the lack of *voice*. Wink (2005) defines *voice* as the use of language to paint a picture of one's reality, one's experience, one's world. It is by developing the *voice* that each individual can reexamine his or her role in the educational process leading to a more equitable place for each person as we learn together how our strengths or assets lead to acquiring *voice*.

A teacher workshop led by Dr. Pizarro provides the background and one example of how a Theory of Social Knowledge initiates *problem-posing*, which through dialogue and reflection begin the empowerment process leading to each individual discovering *voice*. The initial idea for this particular workshop began by bringing together the teacher education staff that works on a federal grant aimed at recruiting and providing workshops for new teachers in the educational program. We began by mapping out the steps:

> *Problem posed: What is the problem or concern?*
> *Reflection: How can we help in effecting change and empowering our students?*
> *Dialogue: What do these changes look like, sound like?*
> *Action: Provide a workshop introducing teachers to challenges of empowerment.*

In order to effect change, a Theory of Social Knowledge requires commitment from all educators and practitioners. The process begins by putting aside ideas of classism, education level, or ethnicity. The facilitator works with the group to bring about the social knowledge needed to begin the transformation.

The first goal of the workshop is to initiate building a circle of trust among the teachers present. As participants develop that trust, they begin breaking down the barriers necessary for change to occur in them, which continues effecting change in others. Then that sense of "identity" begins to emerge.

At a particular moment in the struggle for self-affirmation, when subordinated to and exploited by the ruling class, no social group or class or even an entire nation (or people) can undertake the struggle for liberation without the use of a language. At no time can there be a struggle for liberation and self-affirmation without the formation of an identity, the identity of the individual, the group, or the social class. And to the extent that conflicts increase, experience has taught us that individuals, groups, and social classes end up building walls behind which, in times of struggle or peace, they embrace their identity and protect it. Without a sense of identity, there is no struggle (Macedo, 2006, p. 122).

Reflection and Effecting Change

Once the circle of trust begins, each individual needs to seek personal answers and ask themselves, "Who does education serve and for what purpose?" Wallerstein (2004) further expands on this set of questions by asking, "Does education socialize people to be
objects and accept their limited roles within the status quo, or does it encourage people to question critical issues of the day and fully participate in the social and political life of society?" The workshop introduced our students to changes and solutions leading to empowerment. Each individual needs to find his/her own answers to the questions posed by Wallerstein. As future educators, teachers present in this workshop clearly understood the imperative that they had to find their own *voice* if they were to understand the challenges their students face in the educational setting.

The Workshop in Practice

The workshop, titled *Developing Student Voice Through Everyday Practice,* began with the facilitator presenting a series of questions that students proposed. He began by reminding the teachers that each person needs to see the purpose of his or her own dreams. The results of the workshop would help the teachers understand what he meant by that statement. He began by posing a series of questions and discussing the importance of voice, and the role of identity in a person's life. He asked the teachers to respond in writing to the following question, "What are the questions we ask our students?" They were prompted to do a *quick write* for five minutes, and it was following the quick write that reflection and discussion became blurred as the spirit of change took over the classroom. The participants began to process, connecting personally to the matter of disempowerment. However, this was a slow process. Participants still viewed the discussion as something outside of the classroom, something that happened to somebody else. He then asked, "How many of you had a hard time doing this?" One of the teachers responded by saying, "I have no voice." He then asked "Why?" She responded, "I'm a mother, a teacher, a wife." She had all these roles but no room for her own voice.

It was at this moment that the first "Aha!" started. This part of the process known as *conscientization* starts the process of awakening. Wink (2005) explains with this example,

> Conscientization enables students and teachers to have confidence in
> their own knowledge, ability, and experience….It means that we have
> voice and the courage to question ourselves and the role we are playing
> in maintaining educational processes that
> we do not value. (p.59)

The transformation of self starts as each person begins the self-awareness process, and they respond to the feelings of others. To be aware or conscious of events in our lives prepares us to understand the events of others, and the social knowledge derived from this level of consciousness initiates our journey to find solutions together. The task may sound simple, and teachers may feel that this happens as part of the traditional lecture; however, the traditional workshop lacks the trust-building, rigor, and personal commitment needed to bring about change. *Developing Voice through Everyday Practice* captures how dialogue and reflection work together to create the kinds of changes in the teacher and participants that lead to self-understanding as well as an understanding of others.

The participants at this particular workshop began to uncover the root causes of their students' lack of motivation and lack of voice. They began to examine how they felt and what they needed to do to break the cycle of helplessness. This is only one example of how the Theory of Social Knowledge brings about change. The chapters in this book give other practitioners' stories Examples abound on the theory and the need for multicultural practices in our schools. What is lacking are classroom examples and models to help teachers get started in their own classroom or the practical applications needed to pursue change within the school, the district, or the community. Research enlightens us and helps to create new visions that may lead to lasting change; therefore, if change is to take place, all levels of the educational system must be active participants and committed to that change.

Creating Change

Multicultural Education in Practice: Transforming One Community at a Time illustrates how a program can positively impact the various multi-ethnic communities, schools, and/or districts. Parents, mentors, community leaders, classroom teachers, counselors, and higher education professionals give testimonials of how they applied transformative theory to their practice integrating theory with methodology.

Each chapter demonstrates what needs to happen for transformation to occur in education. The theoretical principles cross various disciplines and pedagogies. Each school of thought adds its tenets composing a *humanizing pedagogy* (Ada, 2001). Other wellknown researchers (Gay, 2000; Villegas, 2002; Darder,1999; Snow & Pang, 2005) speak to the qualities that make up transformative education. Ada (2001) best explains transformative education, pointing out how the various theories fuse, creating a theoretical perspective that demonstrates a deep respect for the individual and also for the group manifestation, including the essential qualities of culture inclusion and language. Creating a program that fosters these principles will look different for each individual or instance; however, the outcome as these authors conclude, creates a better place for students, individuals, and communities.

Questions for Reflection/Classroom Exercise

1. As educators we strive to teach at a level beyond Levels 1 and 2. Why is this difficult? Can you provide an example of how you move a concept through the different levels?

2. Using the graphs on the Theory of Social Knowledge and the Theory of Action, pose a problem or inquiry that you feel requires further investigation. How will these outcomes be different?

Discuss the following quote in groups and present it with a sketch or drawing with very few words. In this conversation, Macedo is discussing with Paulo Freire his ideas on the role of the teacher in the schools.

> The educational task from the perspective of the dominant class is to reproduce its ideology. But the education task that contradicts the reproductionist process cannot be carried out by anyone who opts for the status quo. This task has to be carried out by the educator, who in fact refuses to maintain the inequality inherent with the status quo. The progressive educator rejects the dominant values imposed on the school because he or she has a different dream, because he or she wants to transform the status quo. Naturally, transforming the status quo is much more difficult to do than maintaining it. (Macedo, 2006, p.119)

1. How did your group feel about this excerpt?

2. Does it apply to your particular area or school?

3. Is the dream possible?

4. What does Macedo mean by the status quo?

Chapter 2

Transforming Pancho Villa

by Sergio Perez

Violence is initiated by those who oppress, who exploit,
who fail to recognize others as persons.

Paulo Freire (1996)

Growing up in the border city of El Paso, Texas, one cannot escape the stories of the past, which are filled with heroes, villains, and discrimination. These stories sometimes replicate themselves, bringing to mind one of the most outstanding memories of contempt and injustice that I experienced during my teens. On weekends my father would occasionally take me to the *mercado* across the border and show me the bustling sights and sounds of downtown Juarez, Mexico. He would park the car on the *free* side, and we would walk over to the other side of the border. Finished with our shopping, we would walk back across the border. In one instance, while walking back, my eyes stayed fixed on the woman standing in front of us. She was accompanied by her two children and carried another one in her arms.

At the time I did not know why they caught my attention but later, as an adult with other experiences, I recognized that their sullen but obedient demeanor marked them as humble people, and it was clear English was not their first language. There was a sense of uneasiness in the mother's demeanor that showed as she approached the immigration agent--a sense of laborious impatience, a sense that the unexpected was approaching. Her children were well behaved, and the calloused skin on her hands revealed a woman who was hard-working.

Approaching Pancho Villa

Moments later, the woman and her children were next in line to be questioned about their citizenship by a customs agent, who decided on whether they could cross. I felt uneasy for her. Something told me this woman, held together by her children, was about to go through a severe cross examination, and that this experience was not new to her.

When the agent asked her for her papers, she held out the callused hand waiting for him to take them from her. I waited to see the relief on her face, to replace the worried, cumbersome expression she had been carrying all this time. I glanced over at the officer to see why the consistency of the moving line was disrupted. The features and color of his skin were no different than hers; he was of Mexican descent, almost reminiscent of Pancho Villa, the revolutionary who advocated for the poor and caused havoc for others. He sported a dark mustache and hair that had the stubborn straight brush-like quality I knew well. Obviously, they shared the same ancestry, yet he transmitted an air of power, a demeanor of authority, and became a giant of sorts, confronting this humble, unassuming woman. He massaged his mustached, pondering the documents, observing them with hesitation and suspicion. Regardless, he had no choice; those documents gave her and her children the right to cross. It didn't matter that her Tarahumara-like features and the eccentric coloring of her dress claimed her elsewhere; she had papers signed by a North American dignitary, and this was a fact that he could not ignore. But I guess when you are Pancho Villa you can do anything, and after what must have seemed like an eternity for this poor woman, she heard once more, "I am sorry, but you cannot cross."

This memory continually resonates within me. Perhaps it serves as a reminder of the struggles my own parents went through in their quest for survival. It brings to mind Freire's (1996) words:

> Any situation in which 'A' objectively exploits 'B' or hinders his and her
> pursuit of self-affirmation as a responsible person is one of oppression.
> Such a situation in itself constitutes violence, even when sweetened by
> false generosity, because it interferes with the individuals' ontological
> and historical vocation to be more fully human. With the establishment
> of a relationship of oppression, violence has already begun. (p.37)

I am not sure what the customs agent gained from this encounter. Whatever the reason, the memory of this incident makes me think about who I am as an individual, as a teacher, and how becoming aware of the reality of oppression is the starting point for the transformation to begin.

A Teacher's Journey Begins

For students, the first day of class is always a bit unnerving yet in many ways thrilling. They sit there uneasy and anxious, wondering what the teacher will be like;

what the course will be like, what their peers will be like. It seems that once the students get past that first day, everything falls into place.

After ten minutes or so, the professor to my English course on Multiculturalism still had not arrived, resulting in the comradeship of strangers plotting to claim their rights to the past due "five minute rule." By contrast, it was interesting to see one of our peers stand up and offer to teach the class. Our proposed getaway came to a halt, and briefly, we entertained the clownish idea of an individual with a pair of earrings on each ear and rock-star demeanor, enlightening us with his comedic wisdom. The idea of our sitting there, witnessing this suggestive jester providing us with a mocking performance of a university professor may have erased some of the uneasiness, but it also filled us with awe.

This classmate planted himself at the front of the room and began speaking in a distinct dialect that was clearly English, but out of our cognitive reach. Surprisingly, I was somehow able to decipher fragments of his speech, a discourse addressing diverse issues on multiculturalism. Despite his grandiose and expressive nature, I sensed that I was not the only one dumbfounded by this unassuming yet articulate man who managed to embarrass us with his intelligence. It was not long before we realized this free-spirited John Doe was the teacher. He rambled on for the remainder of class, lecturing in a language that either made you give up, or rise to the occasion. At the next class meeting, half the class had disappeared. This time he stood up there and smiled invitingly, assuring us that the first day's lingo was purposeful in two ways: to recruit persistent, hard-working students, and to help us understand stereotypical misconceptions. Accordingly, the eccentric demeanor of the professor did not jive with the class's stereotypical notion of someone with a Ph.D. The students initially welcomed his unconventional antics, only to feel inadequate later, the moment he told us who he was. In essence, we had formulated an identity based primarily on appearance. Seemingly, our actions were harmless, but the reality that society categorizes you based on what they see is not to be ignored.

I took from the class a lesson that helped me understand the confrontation and the correlation between this professor and the indigenous woman and the customs agent. I found myself questioning how I was perceived and how I perceived others. I realized that many individuals go through life not knowing who they are, and as subjective as the issue of identity is, who one is or who one becomes depends on varying circumstances, including the choices one makes.

Identity Based on Institutionalism

Ironically, the institutions young learners attend strip them of choices; as a result, their identity becomes a self-fulfilling prophecy where fragile young students are led to become what academic institutions define for them. I was enthralled with Multiculturalism and its diverse issues regarding identity, how they define who one is, but through the years, I found that knowing is not enough. Praxis or action needs to follow in order for change to happen.

My first job as a teacher came in the summer and involved tutoring homeless and economically-underprivileged children living in fragile trailer homes or shelters. Many of them were recent immigrants who spoke little English, yet their drive to learn contrasted sharply with the scattered stereotypes that "these" children were vagrants, threatening, and in essence a "lost cause." Society's portrayal of them as "lepers" filled me with assumptions too. I expected these young learners to be tainted, sign-throwing, bandana-wearing tyrants. Despite not owning a television set, fancy clothes or a decent pair of shoes, they showed up in their best attire, wearing natural smiles and presenting themselves with vernacular courtesy. Our meeting was not awkward, but familiar and casual. We played games, read stories, and exchanged hundreds of questions, many concerning the English language. It was not difficult to erase my previous misconceptions of them. More importantly, it made me realize that criticism should be a direct result of lived experiences, not perceived assumptions.

Shortly after the school year began, my students would come to me with cries about "unkind teachers." Initially, I discarded the protest as routine, much like a child complaining about too much broccoli. However, I soon had parents approaching me with the same issues--their children were treated with disregard and neglect. I did not feel sympathy; I felt a sense of helplessness, a sense that despite their potential, despite their hunger for success, the stereotypical assumptions, which routinely defined them, would also marginalize them. I was uncertain about what I could do, and I sensed they were crying out to me for help, but I felt invisible myself. It wasn't quite clear to me why these teachers, these agents of change, were acting so contemptuously, but I knew it had to do with presumptuous labels based on hearsay and misconceptions about language. My sense of helplessness overflowed when state funding for the center was cut off and, with it, the tutoring program.

I was also teaching seventh graders at a Title I school. Naively, I accepted the job with the agreement that I teach a scripted curriculum which, theoretically, was supposed to make teaching easier for me; thus I yielded my enthusiasm to teach these lesson plans.

Notably, Macedo (2006) states:

> A society that reduces the priorities of reading to the pragmatic requirements of capital necessarily has to create educational structures that anesthetize students' critical abilities, in order to domesticate social order for its self-preservation. Accordingly, it must create educational structures that involve "practices by which one strives to domesticate consciousness, transforming it into an empty receptacle.

I wasn't angry, or ignorant, at least not in terms of knowing what I wanted to teach. Behind closed doors, the voice of my multicultural teacher haunted the manner in which I taught. So, I ignored the curriculum and taught the class how I was taught. It wasn't an act of rebellion or defiance; I simply wanted students to hear *my* voice, and in the process find theirs.

Looking back, I am reminded of Thoreau's essay "Civil Disobedience," and the acts of Martin Luther King, Rosa Parks, and Cesar Chavez among many, many others who broke the law in order to uphold a higher, transcendent, law of consciousness and equality. These individuals consciously refused to be defined by the subordinating roles that those in power set out for them. Ironically, my actions were seemingly unconscious, yet I realize now they were truly an act of consciousness because it required me to define myself as an individual. Otherwise, I would simply be conforming to institutionalized, rote frameworks. Macedo's (2006) words rang out and guided my actions:

> Education in cultural action for domination is reduced to a situation in which the educator as 'the one who knows' transfers existing knowledge to the learner as 'the one who does not know.' Paulo Freire's concept of banking refers to this treatment of students as empty vessels to be filled with predetermined bodies of knowledge, which are often disconnected from students' social realities. This type of education for domestication, which borders on stupidification, provides no pedagogical space for critical students. (p.18)

At our class meetings I would protest and question why the curriculum acted as a "one size fits all" prescription. Why couldn't we deviate from the curriculum? Why was theirs the right way and ours the wrong way?

While obtaining my alternative teacher certification, I was introduced to other important works awakening my interest for Piaget and Vygotsky's philosophy on learning. Hernandez (2002) explains,

> When the environment supports the learner, meaning is constructed in accordance with the learner's background knowledge or his or her use of the primary language to explain complex thought. This allows for already existing structure, referred to by Piaget as schemata, to adjust to new information being present in the English language. Schemata are defined as previously acquired knowledge structures that help students process and organize new information and translate it into cognitive and linguistic growth. (p.139)

More importantly, in addition to my own personal research, I was able to connect the idea of schema and a learner's personal experiences to John Dewey's belief of schooling as a social enterprise, one where students learned best through pragmatic experiences. The idea that students brought knowledge into the classroom was enhanced by the idea that students could best learn through other experiences, those in which they could relate and find connections. Consequently, I connected these teaching ideals with my multicultural course and the process of learning about identity through others' stories. It was through storytelling that I learned to read and write, understanding that through others, we learn about ourselves.

Realizing a great number of my seventh grade students came from Spanish-speaking homes, I led them through the process of learning how to read and write, using their own personal experiences and finding a sense of relevancy in literature. I thought about their upbringings, the Mexican culture, modern culture, and the "MTV" generation and about what it was that drove these students. Eventually, I realized my young learners in middle school were different from my young learners at the shelter. Yes, they were of the same ethnicity, spoke at least one of the same languages (Spanish), and both came from families which struggled financially. Regardless, their drives to learn were different. Their experiences of immense hardship, of immigrating, of being sent out to a *tia* or *tio* in order to obtain an Americanized education prompted my sheltered students to feel a sense of urgency, of *needing* to learn. In comparison, the majority of my middle school students, and eventually my high school students, whose parents also came from Mexico, were native-born learners, and their sense of schooling felt more coerced and routine. Despite having access to more resources, their learning was subject to their previous background, upbringing, and experiences.

The following year I found myself teaching high school English, and I went into this environment holding on to the value of identity as my nucleus for teaching. As a result, my teaching reflected group work, narratives, the sharing of stories, art work, and most importantly "tricking" them into learning. It never fails that students ask me why I haven't taught them to "the test." That is not to say I wasn't addressing those skills. I just didn't believe in making the students feel that the learning in the classroom would culminate in a state exam. As a result, I responded to the question put to me by saying, "I didn't realize there was a test." Eventually, they figured out that reading and writing culminate in much more than bubble sheets and formulaic questions. They lost themselves in relating their experiences, and I pushed towards valuing each one of my student's experiences and the resources each one carried within them.

Slipping into Banking Education

Unconsciously, however, I slowly found myself embedding the same oppressive ideals that marginalize students. Professional development or in-service meetings would rarely focus on curriculum development, if at all, placing the majority of the focus on state exams. The pressure to perform and raise numbers surpassed the need to exchange ideas, to tell stories, to value each other as individuals. I had strayed from my own personal beliefs on identity. It no longer mattered what resources a student carried into the classroom. I was on a quest to make good writers better, and inadequate writers adequate. I felt detached and disoriented, making my English Language Learners rewrite their assignments, thinking that was the magic formula to masterful essays.

Of course, nothing I did was entirely detrimental; I still valued their ideas and weighed grammatical errors lightly. In fact, their writing did improve, but they were making improvements through subtle but oppressive means. As a teacher, I had become a dictator, filling their heads with ideas and concepts as I saw fit, as the state exam saw fit. I could sense a detachment in the relationships with my students as individuals, refusing to make learning a transactional process. It no longer mattered who they were because their identity depended on the results of an exam. I had allowed myself to enter the world of banking education. Education thus becomes an act in which the students are the depositories, and the teacher is the depositor. Instead of communicating, the teacher issues communiqués and makes deposits which the students patiently receive, memorize, and repeat. This is the banking concept of education (Freire, 1996).

It wasn't until one of my former students sat in on one of my classrooms that I began to awaken from this capitalistic spell. My visitor called to my attention what I no longer saw. "Mr. Perez, what are you doing!" she told me. "What happened to you? We used to have to so much fun in the classroom." I knew I was faltering as a teacher, even if the administrative agents I answered to thought otherwise. Regardless, I had bought into and conformed to their way of thinking. I found myself being defensive, explaining to her that it was for their own good, that in years past when she was my student, I was a lousy teacher, that I had wasted too much time telling stories and not enough time focusing on the test. But she said something that pierced my sense of consciousness, "Yes, Mr. Perez, we had fun, but it was almost as if you tricked us into learning." I paused, as if trying to remember who I was. The word *tricked* stayed with me, reminiscent of dirty rhetoric, or a persuasive scheme. I began to think that perhaps these test-rooted structures *were* the trick. School textbooks, campus emails, and teacher conversations were inundated with the diction of state assessments.

In terms of assessment scores, it was no secret that our English Language Learners were labeled as the weakest link in the system. Perhaps it was a language issue, but it was also one of identity. It didn't matter that students walked into our classrooms, each one of them ready to tell a story, armed with their history of experiences and background knowledge. They were numbers, or a mere name on a scantron, like the credits on a movie. Sadly, the school culture seemed to strip all of my students of their identity. For my English Language Learners, it didn't matter what events they had lived, what tasks they did well, or what issues they were going through. They truly believed that in order to be successful and be someone, they had to master the English language. It was a culture of language, not content. For the rest of my students, it was a still a culture of language; however, it was a culture of conforming to the language dictated by state assessments. Creativity was muffled by the chants of "exam, exam, exam." Teaching had lost its humanity for me. Its democratic ideals were tarnished, and because incentives (in some instances this meant one's job) depended on scores, I also chanted along with the dictums of state exams and assessment. I had become that individual at the immigration line, disregarding any rights my students had to be someone.

I do not put it lightly when I say that I was very fortunate to participate in a summer institute on Sheltered Instruction. As young as my teaching career has been, my sense of self was constructed of a mosaic of conundrums. In my initial years as a teacher, I cherished students' voices, urging them to challenge me as an educator: "If ever you find an assignment pointless and without value, challenge it, challenge me; if ever you find me inadequate as a teacher, challenge me." Needless to say on more than one occasion my students kept me honest, and I found myself discarding many assignments and replacing them with student discourse. Within a few years, however, those "challenges" no longer stood and neither did those student voices. The system rewired my ideas on what students should learn, and I was drawn into perpetuating it. Participating in a Master's degree program, however, allowed me to reclaim myself and acknowledge that what I was previously doing as a teacher was truly valuable. The chants of sheltered instruction were different; they were those of schema, background knowledge, identity, language, self, and communication. I found myself revisiting my multiculturalism course and conducted research on how to teach students using their voices and experiences. Thomas and Collier's (2001) findings encouraged me to continue searching for ways to help students develop their academic skills, while keeping their language, and striving to excel in English. Baruth (2004) brought me back to the understanding that I knew in my heart was good teaching:

> The more teachers know about and reflect critically upon their teaching, the more effective they will become as educators. The more effective they are, the more successful their students will be in acquiring literate skills they need to be able to read fluently at grade level in order to negotiate the items on the test. Providing a pedagogy that stresses deeper understanding of literacy enables students to go beyond the minimums measured by standardized tests. Students are able to make new meaning of the world around them and therefore begin the process of writing and acting upon the world to change their human conditions. (p. 38)

Reflection Leads to Action

I thought about how that customs agent at the border crossing benefited from keeping a modest woman out--was it taxes, the premise that the image of an American includes Levi's jeans and a Polo shirt, or was it sheer maliciousness? In many ways, her life was in his hands, and so were the lives of her children. To cower and walk away now would be sinful, so it was not surprising to see the image of a woman question authority. He spoke in a language she had heard before. Still she did not understand why he was shaking his head, why he was urging her backwards. Her worried demeanor turned to angst, then into anger and despair. She told him, "*no señor, por favor – tengo papeles, tengo permiso,*" and as she reasoned, one could hear the clearly enunciated sounds of "American," or "U.S. Citizen." The agent's claims that he did not understand Spanish pierced my ears because of their ignorance and hypocrisy, and her anger became my anger. I did not act on my anger. I didn't need to. A Caucasian customs officer, with a stern and determined look, approached the scene as if to put an end to whatever hope was left. He seemed to outrank the other officer and, without asking any questions, laid out his hand asking "*El Genera*" for the woman's papers. The officer conceded and, without hesitation, handed them right back to her, smiled, and with flawless enunciation said, "*Que tenga buen dia señora*." She did not cry the way I had expected; instead, she held her head up high. She had escaped Pancho Villa, and glanced at the clouded twilight of the United States, offering her a sea of uncertainties.

Chapter 3

Unlearning Racism: A Teacher's Journey Leads to School Transformation

by Patricia Perez

To become fully human, we must unlearn
prejudice and bias and become each other's allies.

Ramirez & Gallardo (ix)

Introduction

A society thrives if its members get along and work together to improve that society. Schools are an important part of this process because that is where we learn how to get along with people who are different from us and from those in our immediate families.

Schools want their students to reach their full potential and, in order to do this, students must learn academic skills as well as social skills. If the prevailing educational philosophy of a school is to teach to the STAR Test and raise the API scores, there is no time to teach children about diversity and how to accept all people, no time to learn how to accept those who are different from us, and no time to unlearn prejudice and bias. Schools should be places where racism is confronted and unlearned, where acceptance of all people forms part of an integrated curriculum that is taught and reinforced. Caring, progressive schools do both.

My Journey Begins

Spanish was my first language, and I learned English when I began school. I remember the teacher saying, "Patricia," but I did not know whom she was calling because I only had heard my name said in Spanish. I also remember I had to go to the bathroom, but I did not know how to ask. I was scolded if I spoke Spanish to other children who also spoke Spanish, and I was told the scolding was in order for me to learn English. I felt very alone and confused while in school. This was not the 1940s or 1950s; it was 1961.

We moved to Santa Clara, California, when I was in second grade, and we were one of two Latino families whose children were in the elementary school that I attended. I remember the children making fun of my primary language. They would ask me to say something in Spanish, and they all giggled at the words that flowed from my mouth. They would question me about the Mexican food in my lunch, asking what it was and making disgusted faces.

When I turned ten years old, my mother decided she wanted to become a United States citizen. She began by taking English classes, and she asked my siblings and me to speak only English to her from then on. Unfortunately, I found it easy to let go of speaking Spanish. Since I started my education, I had been told that I should forget Spanish and concentrate on learning English, and now my mother was asking me to do the same. As a result, for many years I only spoke Spanish to my grandmother.

During high school I worked in an electronics firm which employed many Mexican immigrants, and I thoroughly enjoyed reconnecting with my culture and speaking Spanish again. Eventually, my mother and I started an electronics firm, and the majority of the employees were Spanish speakers. Once again, Spanish became the language that I spoke.

Soon thereafter, a friend of mine who had just become a bilingual kindergarten teacher asked if I could volunteer in her classroom. I remember the moment I stepped on the campus, because I heard two women conversing in Spanish, and it was music to my ears. I thought, "Listen to the two *comadres*," and I felt like I finally had found a school where I belonged. I wound up volunteering three times a week.

After volunteering for a year at the school, I realized there was a great need for bilingual teachers, so I decided to become a teacher. I began my teaching in a monolingual fifth grade class until I could be hired as a third grade bilingual teacher. However, I learned that my education did not prepare me to work with children of color. The materials, textbooks, and exams were all aimed for the success of the dominant culture. I refused to lower standards for the ESL students, which meant that I worked extra hours with those students. I held interventions before school, during recesses, lunch, and after school. I worked full-time ten hours a day for two years.

As a third grade bilingual teacher, I saw inequities in achievements between students of color and white students. My solution to the problem was to work part-time and volunteer on my days off in order to close the achievement gap. However, no matter how many hours I put in, the improvements seemed small and inconsequential. After five years of teaching, I began to look deeper into the situation, discovering that the inequities were school-wide. I realized that the problem was bigger than academics alone.

My Leadership Development

After looking critically at the whole picture, I noted that systematic patterns of separation, exclusion, and forms of institutional racism were a dominant factor in this school. I could ignore it and just focus on my class and be the best third grade teacher, or I could take risks and do something about it. I did something about it. I entered a Master's program under a grant in Urban Teacher Leadership, which focused on school change especially for underserved populations. Two colleagues from the same school entered the program with me, and we became teacher leaders for our school site.

Critical Reflection

As part of our studies, we had to decide on a team project. Our professors taught us to look at the world critically, and they challenged us to make a difference at our school site. Paulo Freire's *Pedagogy of the Oppressed*, a text we used in the class, inspired us to act: "The oppressed unveil the world of oppression and through the praxis commit themselves to transformation" (Freire, 2000). We decided we needed to take action and confront the inequities that we were experiencing. One of our assignments became a team project leading us to learn more about institutional racism and its effect on our schools. A few of the facts that we learned guided our work:

The student school population was comprised of 519 students, 44% of whom were white, 29% Latino, 19% Asian American and 8% representing other ethnicities. Approximately 30% of the students received free or reduced-price lunches, and the majority of these were English Language Learners from the bilingual program. Performance and accountability testing showed our last base score was 803.

The Academic Performance Index (API) measures the academic performance and growth of schools in the state of California. Asian American students performed above the statewide performance target of 800, Latinos scored in the 600 range, and Whites scored in the 800 range. Through our research, we found that the staff perceived children of color as underachievers and/or with behavioral problems. White children were perceived to be higher achievers and better-behaved students.

Although it was a bilingual school where 30% of the families spoke Spanish, the office staff could communicate only in English.

- Notices from the office went home in English only, and the library had only a small number of books in Spanish.
- The minority parents were not represented on the committees or at most activities of the school.
- Teachers did not challenge the inequities.

Cultural Action/Implementing Diversity Training

The unfinished character of human beings and the transformational character of reality necessitate that education be an ongoing activity (Freire, 2000). Before any "praxis" or action could take place, discussion and reflection filled the many hours of our planning process. We asked ourselves over and over again, "What is the action that will bring about change?" Our action was to provide monthly staff development sessions to deal with issues of equity, diversity, and institutional racism. We focused on the staff's negative attitudes, assumptions, and beliefs regarding students of color and how they learn. Each of us who worked on these diversity staff development issues brought in information to begin the process of problem deconstruction. We called it "Promoting Positive Interethnic Relations."

To make our diversity training effective, we approached the problem systematically:

- Materials collection, resources, and potential speakers.
- A collection for a video library and books on diversity issues.
- A portfolio of articles relating to diversity and racism.
- Lesson plans available to share with other teachers that would celebrate student diversity and culture.
- Funding for speakers through the district to compensate speakers who could provide a powerful impact on the teachers by discussing issues of inequity or cross cultural themes.

Beginning a school diversity program is a rigorous undertaking. Many tasks require volunteers, and sometimes the person in charge is a volunteer. As the teacher representative on the English Language Advisory Committee (ELAC), I helped plan a school-wide event. Other areas requiring volunteers included help in obtaining funds, working with the PTA, and providing the bilingual parents with a voice at special meetings and school. In addition, as a teacher representative on the PTA Board, it was crucial for me to voice the needs of the students and parents when decisions arose that affected school policies.

Courageous Dialogue

As a PTA teacher representative, I was able to influence school-wide decisions regarding the inequalities between the monolingual and bilingual programs. For example, every year the PTA sent out a Wish List to provide teachers with extras for their classrooms. This list was only in English. At one PTA meeting, I was asked what the response was to this practice, and I had to say that some teachers received a great number of items and others received nothing. I pointed out that the teachers who received very little were in bilingual classes so language was the problem. I said that if we wanted support from all our parents, we would have to make sure they could all read the notices that were sent home. The future PTA president said, "It looks like next year we need to translate all information." From this experience I learned that it is important to be part of the dominant structure and to be vocal about grievances and inequalities in order to effect change.

A lesson I learned that encouraged me to continue talking about inequities that emerge in a school setting involved two particular staff members who approached me asking for my advice. One teacher was worried that she might not have handled a situation well with one of her students in a culturally-sensitive way, and the other teacher asked my advice on how to deal with a student who was racially insensitive to another student. We commiserated and developed strategies for them to use. Having teachers come to me for advice on the subject of racism and inequality made me feel more confident as a leader. Learning about institutional racism, however, takes time to sink in.

Cooperation – A Breakthrough

During one of our diversity training sessions, a fifth grade teacher told me that she found team teaching to be a great way for the kids to get to know each other better. This is exactly what I had hoped would come up because I had been trying for years, without much luck, to get the other primary grade instructors to team teach with the bilingual classes. I complimented the upper-grade teachers for their efforts, and I mentioned that the principal had also noted how well the upper-grade teachers worked together in a team teaching environment. I also took the opportunity to thank Angela, a new third grade teacher in the regular program, for asking me to give her a copy of the Pledge of Allegiance in Spanish. I felt it was important for children to be able to say the pledge and understand the words. This practice would be more meaningful for the children than to repeat words in English, a language that they could not understand.

I thought it was an important step for Angela to celebrate both languages as inherent parts of the school culture, even though she was not teaching in Spanish. Then, many of the teachers started discussing how they could work together and how the regular program could benefit from their learning Spanish. This taught me the importance of open dialogue--we can learn from and encourage each other. The principal was very pleased with the outcome of the meeting. She suggested that at our next staff development session, we encourage all the monolingual program teachers to plan a lesson with the bilingual program teachers during a team-building session, which we did. Angela thanked me for recognizing her and said she felt so proud that she went home and told her husband about the meeting. I am pleased to say that, since that day, I have taught all the third grade classes to say the Pledge of Allegiance in Spanish.

There was still more work to be done at this school site. It was time for teachers to make a decision about continuing the training. When we first started the diversity training, there was resistance from some teachers. Since four of the twenty-six teachers did not attend the trainings, I cannot say that all teachers became more culturally sensitive. However, in the post-staff survey, fifteen out of sixteen responses indicated changes in perceptions (attitudes, assumptions, and beliefs). One comment on the survey said: "I feel my attitude has changed and it made me see that students, people, and cultures are hurting." Sixteen out of sixteen responses indicated an increase in awareness. For example, one response stated, "I've learned that meeting each individual's needs can be quite challenging. Taking the time to know each student, to listen to their stories and concerns can go a long way to build their self-esteem, confidence, and to increase understanding and awareness." While I acknowledge the strides that we have made at our school site, we still need to do outreach with more teachers, and the district needs to value diversity training and implement it in all schools.

Cultural Synthesis

I invited some people from the district office to staff development sessions, and after hearing one very powerful speaker, a person from the district thought it important for our team to deliver diversity training to beginning teachers in the district. I felt honored to be asked to do this – to have people see the value of what I was doing and to want more people to learn how to accept everyone in our society. So far we have done three trainings for Beginning Teacher Support and Assessment (BTSA), and the district has asked us to do more training in the future.

I have seen a great change in myself during the last two years. I have seen myself grow into a bold and socially responsible leader. I have learned that in order to influence change, collaboration is vital. I have learned that in order to transform others, I must first transform myself, and this will be an ongoing, life-long process. I want to continue making changes and helping people to learn to accept each other's differences. Over the last two years, I have found that I have a passion for fighting racism, and I want to continue to be an advocate for social justice.

BEGINNING DIVERSITY TRAINING AT YOUR SCHOOL SITE:

1. Work with the principal to initiate an equity focus.

2. Begin a coffee klatch for staff interested in helping.

    This focus group will volunteer to carry out different tasks.

3. Collect data – See school accountability assignment.

4. Collect materials, videos, books on diversity.

    The Internet will provide a wealth of up-to-date information.

5. Write a pre-survey that meets the needs of your school.

6. Have the teachers fill out a pre-survey.

7. Analyze data.

8. Create an outline for the year based on the school needs

    and an agenda for the monthly staff developments.

9. Measure desirable outcomes.

10. Celebrate.

Questions for Reflection/Classroom Exercises
School Accountability Assignment:

The API scores are found.
1. In a paragraph, describe your school site. Where is it located? What grades are taught there? What languages are spoken? Are students bused in?
2. What are the demographics of the student population?
3. What are the demographics of the teacher population?
4. How many students receive free lunch?
5. What is the latest Base API score for your school?
6. What is the Base API score for Asian-American students?
7. What is the Base API score for Hispanic-Latino students?
8. What is the Base API score for White students?
9. What is the Base API score for African American students?
10. What is the BASE API score for Socio-Economically Disadvantaged students?

In a short paragraph describe what you found, what surprised you the most, and what changes you can suggest to bring about positive changes in your school.

Reflection Questions: Further questions to help your research

1. Find out what the staff's perceptions are about students at your school site.

2. Which groups of students tend to be singled out as behavior problems?

3. Do the referrals and suspensions represent any one group?

4. Is there a group of students who are perceived as low achievers?

5. How do you ensure that your classroom represents all cultures?

6. How are there inequities in the school's resources?

7. How are minority parents represented on school committees at your school site?

8. How are you speaking out against racist remarks?

Chapter 4

Collaboration and Community Transformation Center Stage: When Teachers, Youth and Parents Actively Value Difference

by Rose Borunda and Gwyn Bruch

*Our lives begin to end the day we become
silent about things that matter.*

Martin Luther King, Jr.

Background

Social Justice Theory imparts the understanding that a reconstruction of our social systems must take place in order to evolve into a truly equitable society. From the macro to the micro levels, the transformation that must occur does not mean just doing things differently; it also means that at an individual level, we must recognize one another in a way that fosters improved human relationships from one generation to the next. Conversely, committing to praxis in our social space and in our workplace forces us to examine the very core of why we do what we do. Social justice requires us to evaluate, critically, the realities of our respective worlds, and to ascertain who is included within our worlds and who is not. This critical process forces us to recognize the underlying forces of how it came to be this way and, then, how we come to construct a new reality (Freire, 2000).

One aspect of our reality considered most sacred in our society consists of traditions that are deeply imbedded and enforced by media and culture, and promoted in our educational system. Holidays such as "Columbus Day" and "Thanksgiving" draw mixed reactions. The events on which these holidays were founded resonate positively for some, but they also exclude and discount a vast number of diverse voices within a society historically grounded on conquest, colonization, violence, and slavery (Loewen, 1999). Even today, the controversy surrounding "Columbus Day" and "Thanksgiving" compels us to question whose "story" is being promoted at the exclusion of other perspectives.

The benefit of having multiple historical perspectives on the forces that have shaped our present leads to enhanced understanding of one another at the cognitive and affective levels. The need for a new nation which recognizes and acknowledges a mosaic of historical occurrences must not be minimized; at the same time, the accuracy, context, and cause for celebration of such events from our past to our ongoing practices of today call for critical examination--if we are to evolve as a whole. For this reason, we celebrate those modern-day heroes who critically examine our "traditions." For example, by examining some of the early portrayals of John Brown, a white man who fought to abolish slavery, we see that he was branded a "mad man" for his convictions (Zinn, 2001). The challenge for educators today is re-visioning the course of long-held historical traditions and beliefs, challenging those beliefs, and, in the process re-creating more inclusive venues that promote greater understanding among various communities and community members. This chapter will highlight the evolutionary work of one educator in the hope of modeling steps that others may follow.

The Bear Awakened

As a former practicing junior and high school guidance counselor, my experience with activism and social justice has long focused on working within the school's community. Upon completing my doctorate degree, I secured a position as a counselor educator at a university, which required that I relocate my family for a better commute for my husband and myself. We selected a nearby college town as our new community, as it appeared to offer all that was needed to enhance our daughter's development, while allowing us to enjoy the amenities that come with living in a college town. Subsequently, from reading one of my own textbooks assigned to my graduate students in Multicultural Counseling, I was shocked to discover that a Vietnamese student had been murdered on the high school campus that my daughter was now attending (Gibbs, Huang, 2003). The attack was racially motivated. This revelation marked the beginning of a journey in advocacy that would find me on the outside of the school that my daughter attended.

My growing awareness of the need for collective action within my new community was fueled by what I read daily in the local newspaper as well as accounts from my daughter and her friends. After teaching about social justice principles at the university, I would read about ongoing acts of racial hatred and ignorance committed by my fellow community members. In our first year of living in this community, my daughter returned from school one day and reported witnessing a brutal fight between two other Latinas, one for whom it was her first day of school. This confirmed for me that even in supposedly progressive college-town communities, those who are marginalized will continue to be marginalized unless they are engaged and valued (Freire, 2000).My daughter's reports of the disproportionate number of students whom she witnessed seeing in the suspension room, engaged in gang affiliation or other school or community related problems only pointed to a repeat of what I had to work actively to undo in this and other communities where I served as a school counselor in school districts in the East Bay area.

The implications of my daughter's experiences in completing her last four years of mandatory education would ultimately have a tremendous impact on my own community involvement. It was not enough, now, to teach classes at the university and draw from past experiences of enacting social justice strategies to ensure better outcomes for traditionally marginalized communities where gang affiliation, teen pregnancy, parental disengagement and educational disconnection were common. A series of events, including eye-opening awareness of exclusionary social structures (Diller, 2004) and ongoing attacks on people of color in "my community," ultimately forced me out of the margins and into public view.

Hate Crime or Kids Being Kids? Which Traditions are Normal?

My husband and I were awakened at 3:00 am by the ringing of the phone and the sound of car horns honking outside of our home. It was the final day of Homecoming Week, 2003, at my daughter's school. My husband and I stepped outside our home to discover that carloads of high school students (they were wearing masks), under cover of night had scrawled profanity laced messages on our driveway, the street, and the sidewalk. Our trees were completely covered with toilet paper and garbage was strewn across our front lawn.

Though the attack was directed at our daughter, our collective nature generated a response to this attack as a violation against our entire family. Fortunately, our daughter was not at home. She had spent the night consoling a friend whose father passed exactly one year ago. My husband and I spared her the news of this hateful act by local youths by cleaning up every trace of it before the sun rose. While doing so, we discussed the nature of a community in which its youths spent considerable time and effort committing acts of hate. In our hometown, it was not atypical for youth to "toilet paper" the homes of others, but these acts were generally considered benign and good-natured. We discovered that the intent of this same act, by the youths of our adopted hometown, though not tolerated by school officials, was usually committed with parental knowledge.

The historical implication of attacks on Latinas with messages that included sexual connotation is deeply rooted in our psyche. To us, this was a reenactment of ongoing, disrespectful behaviors by one cultural group against another. When I sought restitution and intervention from the police and from school officials, I discovered that such acts were not only "common" but also downplayed by several members of the larger community as "kids will be kids." Seeing the savage behavior of the community in which we lived, and the complacency that condoned it, compounded our sense of outrage. We started looking at alternative schools for my daughter's senior year; meanwhile, the spirit of the bear in me was called to action.

Community Connections

What was revealed to me in the process of coming to grips with the nature of the community was the pervasiveness of its social/emotional deficiencies (Goldman, 1995), especially how people related to one another. Certainly, there were those who had been working for social justice within this community long before my family moved here, but their impatience with the lack of change over the years (marked by the tragic murder of the young man on the high school campus) only confirmed for me that deeply-rooted attitudes and intolerances were perpetuated from one generation to the next.

As a former counselor working to eradicate the conditions leading to gang affiliation and youth disconnect, I was now called into community activism. One of my graduate students, Cathy Sacks, introduced me to Dr. Jann Murray-Garcia, the President of Blacks for Effective Community Action (BECA). Dr. Murray-Garcia and her husband, a practicing medical doctor, were intent on raising their two young children in this community, and they were especially determined not to be run out of town as other people of color had ultimately been forced to do after numerous acts of hostility were directed against them. From the margins of the activism, I began organizing and presenting at various venues within "our" community. My daughter, also, made the ultimate decision to fully engage herself in improving the climate of her school community so that future generations would benefit from the collective efforts of those who were determined to make a difference.

Ultimately, I came to know Gwyn Bruch, the drama teacher at my daughter's high school. Gwyn and I were both in attendance at a community-wide presentation in which data reported from Youth in Focus, a research group coordinated by Dr. Murray-Garcia, revealed disparate outcomes for students of color within the school system. These were outcomes common in most communities, yet the response to those who heard the scathing report from the youth scholars led to the questions that Gwyn would now pose to students at her school. Ultimately, this served as the catalyst for change. In the next section, Gwyn Bruch explains what led her to take action, the kind that Freire refers to "conscientization" or coming to conscience.

Acts of Transformation: "Songs of Ourselves"

This is my fourteenth year as a drama teacher at this high school. I have attempted to provide venues for all students to feel included. Though most drama productions are written by Euro-Americans about Euro-American experiences, I have implemented color-blind casting in which even the role of Helen Keller, in a play about her life, was played by a Sri Lankan. After I heard the Youth in Focus Report, the outcomes spoke loudly to me and were too real to deny. They forced me to take a look at the racial and ethnic composition of students in my program: We were not representative of the ethnic/racial diversity of our high school. This moved me to the next step which was to attend our school's Climate Committee where I knew there would be students of color in attendance who could safely speak about these issues. It was there that I asked for their feedback about our drama program. One student responded, "I came to your auditions in the fall, and was very excited about getting involved, but I was told by a member of your inner circle that I shouldn't bother to audition (because I was Chinese)."

Other students of color chimed in, and I heard statement after statement revealing their feelings of alienation and exclusion. I wanted to scream with frustration. This was not how I wanted my department to be perceived or to operate. It was painful to hear that people were reluctant to come and audition. More so, it was more painful to hear that one of my students who represented herself as being in my inner circle was overtly cruel and exclusionary.

Taking Action: Inviting Change

My next step was to bring this sentiment to my Drama Advisory Board (DAB). This group consists of a group of eight to twelve students who have demonstrated extraordinary commitment to the program. They make policy for the department and do all the grunt work to make the production a success. Since this program is for the students, I needed the students to guide the program.

I shared with the advisory body what their peers at the School Climate Committee candidly revealed to me. For the next hour they expressed their own sense of outrage. They were taken aback by how one person could purport to speak on behalf of students in DAB (who were white) and use the unspoken yet very real solidarity of race that exists in this society to exclude others. A student had revealed the color line and used it to disadvantage others. The capricious manner of this maintained separateness prompted further discussion by the members of DAB who were now forced to confront the reality of cliques and racial and ethnic barriers on their campus. What, if anything, were they going to do to address these realities?

For me, as a drama teacher, the realization was that using color-blind casting alone did not create inclusion for students who have been marginalized on our school campus. This situation moved me to examine more deeply the true and genuine forms of inclusion to the exclusion of others. Given the cultural context of the traditional productions I introduced, I came to the conclusion that I had been asking people of color to fill the roles of Euro-Americans. This meant that I was conveying to students of color that they could be on stage only if they pretended to be what they weren't…white. How then, am I to create inclusion and respect for diversity if I am only providing venues that ask "others" to fit our stories and our roles, but not theirs? The answer was to bring their stories to the stage and to promote their own heritage in a way that allowed them to be who they truly are. This became the impetus behind "Songs of Ourselves."

The Transformation Affects Students and Community

As a white woman, I ask myself, "Am I qualified to produce and direct a multicultural/ethnic production?" I had to get past my feelings of inadequacy; yet I refused to let that stop me. I am in a role that impacts the venue for what is presented and avails the stage in a way that can potentially honor who people are, for themselves, without asking that they compromise their true identity. My own value system told me that whatever I did necessitated doing so in a respectful way. At this point, I turned to those from the various communities who could provide the access and knowledge that I needed to create inclusion on my stage.

Gathering from multiple sources—including books on fairy tales and talking with the representative elders--I decided to introduce fairy tales and legends from various cultural groups into dramatic production. One of the fairy tales from the Brazilian Rain Forest presented multiple realities of spirits and animals as characters, a production that could only be done through music and dance. Music has a powerful connection at the most visceral level. It is also central to culture. As an artist, I considered the place that music has in cultural heritage and in representing the uniqueness and beauty of different cultures. Also, music engages the audience in ways that words cannot, and it is the vehicle for transmitting the essence of culture, for the enrichment of the players and the audience.

In putting out the call for what I needed, I discovered that making personal contact with each ethic cultural group on campus was more difficult than I envisioned. In some cases, various community groups representing different cultures came to us. People connected with Youth in Focus, including Dr. Jann Murray-Garcia and Dr. Rose Borunda, and they generated initial interest and support from cultural experts. Then, I initiated my own outreach to those who were connected with groups that would more fully represent other world cultures. Approaching cultural readers with a genuine humility, I asked them to share their expertise.

The role of these experts was to: (1) fill in the gaps, and (2) offer a different perspective. Having worked professionally, I had a wide circle of experts to draw from. This is where resourcefulness serves as an asset.

From the outset I saw myself as the facilitator rather than as the director in the traditional sense. My profession dictates that a director should have complete artistic control over every aspect of a production, yet here, it was my role to set the creative wheels in motion and step back. I focused my energy on ensuring that basic drama principles of acting and staging were adhered to at all times. Because we were working at such a fundamental level, however, I used this opportunity to empower my advanced students by allowing them to serve as directors.

Praxis: Transformation in Action

The actual experience of producing "Songs of Ourselves" was chaotic, frenetic, but also fun. There was a special delight and energy when bringing students onto the stage who projected a tough exterior demeanor on the campus but who also projected innocence in their performance onstage. I purposely did not spend a tremendous amount of time hammering away at drama fundamentals. There was a beautiful, fragile quality to the raw nature of the performances. I am a control freak, so delegating is not easy. I consider it an enormous victory that I gave over the directing of most of my scenes to my advanced students. It required that I stay on my side of the fence and allow my students to figure out how to work with their casts. I could not sacrifice all of my standards, though. For instance, I brought in a friend, my mentor, as a director and a drama teacher, to guide the conceptualizing of a particularly raw piece that required unique staging and direction.

The reaction to the change in venues from my colleagues has been mostly neutral. One teacher colleague stated after hearing about the production from various students, "I envy you because of the passion that you bring out in these kids."

There is a natural energy that surrounds my room and, with the change of production, there was an energizing that prompted a quantum leap in my program. On the other end of the spectrum, there was some reaction by colleagues who expressed concern over students missing class time. In the opinion of some of our staff, our program does not have merit, like the ski team and other sports teams where it is acceptable for students to regularly miss classes. Having to assert the time I needed to make this production work did receive some criticism. But, in the end, I see it as a deeper investment in the relationship building that I already do with students as I walk across campus reaching out to them while they congregate within their own segregated groups. In the end, the relationships are what will keep them connected to our school in a meaningful way. The writer gives her reactions as a parent and community member in the passage that follows.

Reflections from a Parent

The impact on students who have traditionally experienced marginalization was now not only in the forefront, but the students were also taking on lead roles that represented their respective cultural groups. My daughter auditioned for "Songs of Ourselves" and was cast in the role of *Xihuatl*, a Mexica princess, who is portrayed in a famous Aztec legend. Serving also as co-director for this particular vignette allowed her to work more closely with a respected elder of our community and former professional performer with the Mexican Ballet Folklorico Troupe, Angelbertha Cobb. The respect and honoring of our own heritage, being promoted through "Songs of Ourselves," encouraged my daughter to draw upon the knowledge and expertise of this cultural expert who not only provided the legend but who also taught my daughter a song that Mrs. Cobb had professionally recorded in the early 1940's. After learning the song, "*Tonantzin*" (Mother Earth), in Nahuatl and the accompanying dance, my daughter was able to share what she learned with other students from her own and different cultural backgrounds that, otherwise, would not find an audience on most high school stages.

As a parent of color who had seriously considered pulling my daughter from this school for her final year, I now saw that she was contributing to an environment that fostered emotional and social growth for all. My observations as a parent convinced me that my daughter's role would ultimately serve the community in providing the context through which our youth could critically understand the nature of misconceptions, stereotypes, and alienating cliques. Gwyn was carefully creating a safe place where students from all walks of life could build relationships and overcome the negative association of "difference," while learning to honor and respect their own cultural heritage. The one area of disagreement that we had was when Gwyn vetoed the participation of a strawberry blond student in the initial piece in the program, but I assured her that our culture demands inclusion. Gwyn was adamant, however. She felt, at this juncture, that it was important that this first piece feature only students who represented the culture in physical appearance so that local school children who are from this cultural heritage could see that their heritage is rich, special, and worthy of great pride.

The transformation was taking place at multiple levels. One student of color who was involved for the first time in dramatic production expressed how he perceived himself prior to his involvement with "Songs of Ourselves": "My skin is always two shades too dark." After his active participation in multiple roles he stated," I'm glad I joined drama and was a part of the play. I don't know why I didn't do it before because I really enjoyed it."

Previously noting how race and color contributed to exclusion, this student's positive experience not only diminished these marginalizing factors but also gave him a place to belong and to participate in the fullest. I asked Gwyn what she felt made the difference in creating an atmosphere where students working on the play came to value one another. She responded,

I had to create inclusion of all students and to create an atmosphere where everyone was valued; every full cast rehearsal in the theater started in a circle holding hands. As a practice, all students were asked to look around the circle and see the faces of others. This created a meaningful way to promote connection and relationship. Then, students had to approach three different people and introduce themselves. We also had one meeting in which we did a team building activity.

The transformation within the drama department became apparent. Something new and evolutionary had taken place, but what Gwyn did and what she will explain in the next section took me by surprise.

New Beginnings: The Decision to Usurp "The Spring Musical"

I received tremendous accolades from the community for "Songs of Ourselves." This was the most heartfelt support I have ever received about a production. Though the final product of "Songs of Ourselves" was not up to my polished standards, the reaction to the quality of raw talent made it foundational to future performances. This contributed to my letting go of the past and embracing the natural evolution of the drama program. The surrounding energy moved me to take the next step: to pull the traditional "American" spring musical, "Carousel," replacing it with a show that would continue to include the people who were now engaged on my stage. I felt sure and happy about this critical decision, but the response of others was not quite as enthusiastic. One student exclaimed that my decision to pull the traditional spring musical to an inclusive multicultural venue had, "Flipped My World! We already did something for them." Another resistant student attempted to diminish the quality of "Songs of Ourselves" by stating, "It wasn't worthy of a 4th grade class."

There were only two students who expressed strong objections, and I saw the resistance for what it was. I had attacked their privileged status as seniors who expected to be center stage. Their resistance came from a very personal and egocentric perspective. Initially, about four or five juniors were swayed by the negative senior energy because it fed their uncertainty. It's easier to put on a show where the script is written and all roles are prescribed. What I was proposing had no precedence. It was not so much that they thought this was a bad idea; they were intimidated by their strong friends and scared with no script, no score, etc. The chaos of the fall would be repeated on a larger scale. "Why are you doing this to us?" they asked.

On the other hand, I felt support from those students who were centered enough as people, and could see the new picture that was emerging. The newcomers were excited, though, and some people that I respect were excited as well. In the end, if drama directors and teachers decide to embark upon such a transformative endeavor, I advise that they assess their students' feelings first. If resistance is real, deal with it head on. I spent hours privately counseling my strongest senior, addressing her deeply personal insecurities. At our next meeting I was stronger than they had ever seen me, and while I gave them the choice to participate, letting them know they would all be included, I also made it clear that I would not tolerate obstruction or under-the-radar divisiveness.

Setting the Stage: A Truly Equitable Society

Initial attempts to create a new production involved the recruitment of two students to serve as student writers. Each had their own perspective, but I saw this as an advantage rather than as a detriment to the creation of a script. When we met initially to determine the direction of this unnamed and yet to be determined musical production, the first thing we had to ask ourselves was, "What do we want the musical to say?"

To ground us, I recruited a professional playwright who listened to our ideas. In the end he affirmed our vision, which was to produce an ensemble show similar to "Chorus Line." Our initial plans were to have principal/feature roles for up to thirty students. We held auditions without a script to see what talent came knocking at the door. After wide publicity, word of mouth, posters, and friendship circle recruitment, we had sixty students try out, significantly more than our usual forty. Since ensemble participation does not require auditions (I believe that every high school student should be in a play), this opened up the door for an even broader circle of students to become involved in one form or another.

We planned to tailor the script to the particular participants, and we were looking beyond the usual suspects to tell a story, participate in a short improvisation, dance, and sing a song of their choice. Our challenges appeared immediately. Our strongest male actor, around whom the first script had been shaped, did not show up for auditions. After significantly adjusting our concept based on the talent of a new face at auditions, that boy withdrew. After learning that one of the themes addressed in the play would touch upon homosexuality, he expressed his own discomfort with topics that were not condoned in his home. We now veered in a third direction.

With the strength of resourcefulness, we drew upon the talent of two graduates from our high school, both accomplished playwrights now majoring in theatre at NYU. They met with our two student writers and, again, the question resounded, "What do we want the musical to say?" We knew we didn't want to limit the production to one particular topic that would restrict us from addressing a variety of issues that affect all students. During this production phase, I caught myself wanting to throw in ideas. I learned, however, to be quiet because while my thoughts held merit in a theatrical sense, they were not valid to the reality of the students. My commitment was to empower the students to speak their own truths. I pulled back, trusting them to know what is real and give it life. Ultimately, they chose to address the theme of alienation, which included academic and social pressure, competition, alienation, identity, sexuality, stereotypes, racism, under-the-radar bullying, dreams, and aspiration. And, while like its predecessor in the fall, this piece did not have a name for most of the rehearsal period, we finally settled on "Remember Tomorrow."

In creating "Remember Tomorrow," we started with the idea of identifying groups and cliques on campus and the individual characters that comprised each group. Then, we created a line of scenes, following the students at a high school, similar to ours, through a typical day. Featured and principal actors were assigned to groups, with one group labeled "unaffiliated." They were then assigned certain characteristics and given certain circumstances, such as your parents are going through a divorce, and "they don't want to hear about it." Some actors played characters somewhat close to their own personalities while others played characters far removed from themselves.

Each member of the cast was asked to write a character description, taking socioeconomic status into consideration such as lifestyle, family make-up, personal likes and dislikes, etc. I encouraged the students to look around them and suggested that, most likely, their character would be a mixture of people they might know and that they might be pulling material and using characteristics taken from their friends. This gave them the opportunity to examine the behaviors and characteristics of those around them, making the assignment more concrete and immediate. One particular student responded to her given circumstances by declaring, "That's me! This is who I am." This goes back to the understanding that if students can see themselves on stage and be who they are, then they are being affirmed in their own world and in their own reality. Their collaboration, based on deep mutual respect, commitment to giving voice to the sometimes sordid often painful truths of everyday high school life, and highly developed appreciation for the irreverent and profane, was a delight to experience. Ultimately, a few other students got involved in last minute additions – adding to those who felt significantly invested in this project.

For the first six weeks of rehearsals, we had only the sketchiest of scripts and no music, which made full-cast rehearsals awkward. I was forced to use all my inner resources as well as exhausting my bag of "drama teacher tricks." I lost a few of the least flexible cast members during this period, but the new faces who appeared were attracted by unusual goings-on outside the drama room--involving lots of noise and laughter, which more than compensated for our losses.

Mid-February, just a month out from opening, we met with a former faculty member, a strong advocate for drama and current staff member of our local suicide prevention organization, to discuss the ramifications of centering our script around suicide. She provided us with valuable information and honest, if disheartening, feedback, pointing out that our invisible boy was theatrically uninteresting and, more importantly, that any way we played it, we ran the risk of inspiring some vulnerable young person to attempt suicide. So we decided against the suicide angle in the production, thus removing the lynchpin from our plot. In a testament to the resilience of our team, within thirty minutes my students had solved the problem by replacing suicide with an accident.

To ensure a modicum of support, most importantly from our administration and also from groups I thought might be offended by the content of our production, I distributed scripts to a variety of students and administrators. The input from others who might have a more conservative view of our work was crucial to stemming public outrage. The administration is generally on the front line in dealing with irate parents. As a result of the solicited feedback, we removed language that was most offensive in exchange for retaining controversial content.

At the outset, I did not think we had the time to write original music, so we spent several fruitless weeks exploring alternative routes. At this point, my beloved colleague, Chris Lee, a social studies teacher and brilliant pianist/musician who had acted as musical director for several previous productions, declared his intention to write his own songs. Chris said, "Explain to me the character, the situation, and what you want the song to say and I'll write it." And he did! Bringing added depth and clarity to the show with his powerful melodies and insightful lyrics, Chris Lee tailored music for individual singers, then spent innumerable hours in his home recording studio creating backing tracks.

With three weeks to go, we introduced hip-hop choreography sessions via a charismatic professional choreographer. I flew in a dear friend, Carlos Mendoza, whom I had known when he was a student at our school, and, now a professional entertainer in Los Angles. Carlos was heavily involved in Latino theatre. I originally thought of Carlos as a hook to draw in Latino students – a group that has proven to be the most reluctant to get involved in my productions. Ultimately, Carlos helped us clarify important production issues with the professional, unclouded eye of an impartial observer. He quickly became caught up in the energy of the students, staging the opening and coaching several scenes. I also brought in from Oakland an African-American actor who coached the "ghetto group," believing they needed someone who could validate their experiences with his own life story. His goal was to work with the actors' enunciation in order to preserve their characterization while ensuring that audiences who were not in tune to their style of speech could understand. On opening night, I stood on stage with our composer, an Asian; our choreographer, an African-American; and our co-director, a Latino; and a multi-ethnic/multicultural cast of seventy-four young people (by far the largest cast we have ever had).

What We Gained From "Remember Tomorrow"

"I feel renewed and energized."

Affirmed by the response that I got from the cast, the school and the community, I saw that all the pain we went through to get to where we are now was worth it. Today, our program is different. The sense of ownership and responsibility for creating something important is beyond wonderful. There is a depth of satisfaction that I have never felt before.

On a larger scale, we took discernible steps toward breaking down barriers. Students had to work together. Everybody was learning side-by-side. They were learning about themselves, and they were learning about others. They walked in someone else's shoes for nine weeks. It was a powerful, healing experience in that students were able to use the stage to convey to the rest of the world how alienating and isolating life can be. Furthermore, this process of staging and performance revealed how exclusion, alienation, and isolation are created and perpetuated through a myriad of small but meaningful incidents, remarks, and slights every day. The audience was not spared the reality of what it feels like to be a high school student, today. At the end of each production, the students then engaged in real dialogue with the audience about their reality, taking the first step toward opening the discussion on how to get to a more harmonious and inclusive world.

The Promise of Positive Change held within "Remember Tomorrow"

The transformation off stage, which resulted from making "Remember Tomorrow," has given me impetus for real and lasting change. Next year we plan to produce this show again, after considerable revisions made without pressure and tension-filled urgency. We intend to publish a script designed to be moldable for schools with different social hierarchies and divisions. I am also looking through a stack of professionally-published scripts that are more inclusive of a wide range of voices and realities. The task of undertaking such an endeavor, of making one's stage a platform for social justice where difference is valued, is not an easy task, but it is a rewarding and transformative one.

Questions and Reflections/Classroom Exercises

1. Discuss with a partner or small group the events in this chapter. Has anyone in the group had similar high school experiences? What were the particular circumstances? What are the challenges?

2. At your particular school, what are some of the issues that would prevent a teacher or teachers from creating change of the sort seen in this chapter?

3. If you began a similar effort in your school, what would be the challenges? List the challenges and possible way of meeting those challenges.

Chapter 5

Honoring and Sustaining Heritage Languages: Strategies for the Non-Bilingual Teacher

by Zaida McCall-Perez

Introduction

The field of multicultural education is fortunate to be able to draw on the work of a number of inspired educators and researchers (Banks, 2001; Cummins, 1989; Nieto, 2008) who have advanced theoretical frameworks to guide practitioners in developing the how and what of multicultural practices in schools. The Multicultural Education (MCE) principles introduced by Banks, Cummins, and Nieto/Bode (2008) have gained acceptance in many organizations and learning communities who have committed to embracing diversity as a fundamental principle. James Banks' (1994) theoretical framework is discussed in Chapter One, but it contains no explicit reference to bilingual*ism or* bidialectical-*ism*. Although Nieto and Bode (2008) mention language in their Multicultural Framework, neither they nor James Banks fully integrate the linguistic equity issues related to heritage language that are the focus of this chapter.

This author wishes to draw attention to bilingual*ism*, defined as the skill to use two languages in all situations, not Bilingual Education, defined as a school program for selected students which uses a students' primary language to bridge to instruction in the language of the host country, in our case, English. Bilingual Education thrived, and then endured, decades of political controversy prior to the passage of chilling legislation in multiple states, such as California's Proposition 227 in 1998. The dialogue regarding bilingualism as a national resource which peaked politically during the cold war era of the 60's has lost its political shine, but not its actual value. There is ongoing international advocacy promoting linguistic human rights to counter worldwide discrimination based on language (Skutnabb-Kangas and Philipson, 1995). And last but not least, a considerable body of literature about the cognitive benefits of bilingual*ism* continues to emerge (Adesope, Lavin,Tompson and Ungerleider, 2010; Bialystok, Craik, Luk, 2008; Gutierrez-Clellen, Calderon, Weismer, 2004). This author suggests that it is time to shift the dialogue about schooling to include bilingual*ism* within the theoretical frameworks for Multicultural Education.

A rich national resource for languages is the immigrants and children of immigrants who speak them. After an immigrant family's loss of the original first language, it is not uncommon for subsequent generations to lament this loss and attempt to re-capture their heritage language(s). It is for this reason that this author chooses to use the term "heritage language" rather than terminology currently in use such as: primary language, home language, foreign language, world language, and/or global language. Almost any language in today's world is, or has been, the ancestral or heritage language of a U.S. citizen.

Honoring heritage languages falls well within the theoretical framework of Multicultural Education proposed by Banks (2001) and Nieto and Bode (2008) without a requirement for Bilingual Education Programs per se. The explicit inclusion of heritage language reflects this author's perspective that individual and societal benefits of "bilingualism" serve as both as an end in themselves, and as a means to an end, Multicultural Education. In the spirit of *Multicultural Education in Practice*, this chapter presents theory and rationale for inclusion of heritage languages (HL) within the Nieto/ Bode (2008) Multicultural Education framework and ends with practical strategies that teachers who do not speak the language(s) of their students can utilize to engage and support the bilingualism of their students in their learning process.

Including Heritage Language in Nieto/Bode (2008) Multicultural Education Framework

The Multicultural Education theoretical framework developed by Sonia Nieto and Patty Bode (2008) encompasses a 5 stage continuum: (1) monocultural (2) tolerance (3) acceptance (4) respect (5) affirmation, solidarity and critique. This author has developed a parallel framework focusing on heritage language shown on the following page:

Figure 5.1
Bilingualism within the Theoretical Framework
for Multicultural Education

Monocultural	• Replace (substitute heritage language(s) with the language of the majority culture. • Policies promote only English langauge usage for classroom interaction and academic tasks.
Tolerance	• Allow, without punishment, the expression of heritage languages at time, and in spaces, where they do not infringe on others in any way.
Acceptance	• Compliance with (CA) state law, federal regulations and case law, e.g., providing translators and translations where 15% are speakers of a single heritage language. • Nothing volitional beyond what is required
Respect	• Voluntary school practices and policies that respect global languages and cultures beyond legal compliance, e.g., facility signage, use of heritage language for some academic purposes is permitted.
Affirmation, Solidarity and Critique	• Dual-Language instruction beginning in elementary, heritage and global language instruction at secondary for native and non-native speakers aimed at achieving biliteracy. • Use of an official "Seal of Biliteracy" and public acknowledgement • Local district policy exists regarding linguistic rights of teachers and students.

Categories from *Nieto & Bode (2008);* content adapted and enhanced by *McCall-Perez (2010)*

The **Monocultural** category is an easy equivalent of monolingual schooling – a place where there may be explicit edicts about not using any language other than English for either official or informal purposes. Many of today's adult immigrants recall that in their own elementary educations, they were told "don't speak Spanish" and even punished when they did. In a monocultural school setting, the language policy – explicit or by default – would be to teach English as quickly as possible period. Mastery of English would be required in order to participate in mainstream school activities. If a middle or high school were divided into "houses" or "academies", students just learning English would not belong to one until they had a sufficient level of English. Loss of the heritage language would not be viewed as a matter of any concern. An underlying expectation might be that English Learners ought to be able to acquire English by participating in the mainstream without any special considerations – strategies or materials – that differ from those used with all students.

Tolerance. According to Nieto/Bode (2008) "tolerance might be viewed as having to bear linguistic and cultural differences as the inevitable burden of a culturally pluralistic society" and as school programs that "do not build on differences but rather replace them – for example, ELL programs" (p 426). An example might be that when parents who speak non-English languages come to the school for an event, school staff and parents may feel obliged to tolerate one or more non-English languages for that occasion, but experience it as a burden. That a child who was once fluent in a heritage language graduates from high school as a monolingual English speaker is an example of replacing differences rather than building on them. For this author, tolerance suggests that there is no explicit prohibition – no rule posted on the wall, but also no overt gestures of acceptance either.

Acceptance in Nieto/Bode's (2008) words are "programs that acknowledge students' languages and cultures are visible" and "might include a transitional bilingual program ...at least until they are mainstreamed into an English-language environment" (p 426). She further notes that "parents' native languages might be used for communicating with them through newsletters." In a high school, Nieto/Bode (2008) note that possibly "a variety of languages are taught" (429).

However, in California, some of these indicators of 'acceptance' have already been legislated, making it difficult to distinguish what is embraced voluntarily from what might be reluctant or resentful compliance with current regulations. For instance, communicating in parents' native languages is a matter of compliance with current California Education Code that requires schools and districts to provide written communications in any languages spoken by 15% or more, of the school attendance area. At the secondary level budget cuts in all non-core curricular areas, combined with an increase in basic skills requirements for designated "school improvement schools" under No Child Left Behind (NCLB), have contributed to a reduction in global, previously known as "foreign language" courses. In California, this author envisions that true measures of 'acceptance' are reflected in more subtle, and voluntary evidence.

Respect as Nieto/Bode (2008) define it is "to admire and hold in high esteem" and suggests that it might also mean "offering programs of bilingual education that employ students' native language not only as a bridge to English but also throughout their schooling" (p427). Respect, then, for Nieto/Bode as well as for this author, is more pro-active than 'acceptance.' As noted in the previous paragraph, this author identifies the most pro-active indicators of 'respect' as culturally and linguistically subtle and caring forms of outreach that are likely to exceed the established legal minimums. Compliance with regulations alone does not differentiate between a pro-active multicultural school community and a resentful, or reluctantly compliant, one.

In a post-227 California, traditional Bilingual Education has been capped at second grade. There is a slow but steady resurgence of Alternative Bilingual, Dual-Immersion programs beginning at the early elementary level. At the secondary level, the beacons of pro-active linguistic respect are emerging in the form of heritage language classes for native speakers and global language classes for non-native speakers. Spanish for Native Spanish Speakers and Spanish for Non-native Speakers trends strongly support this author's position that a new dialogue about bilingual*ism,* possibly associated with linguistic rights*,* and not simply Bilingual Education Programs is timely.

Another genuine voluntary indicator of the multicultural 'respect' stage is evident when bilingual and/or heritage language children's literature can be found in use in general education classrooms and available in local school and community libraries, not just in designated Bilingual Education Program classrooms or courses. Some multicultural, multilingual schools have pro-active signage indicating "office" in English and in the heritage languages of the school community, a subtle welcome not required in the law. Further evidence of multicultural 'respect' can also be seen in local efforts by the school communities to not only seek the inclusion of immigrant parents in mainstream activities, but also in the participation by the mainstream community in celebrating events of importance to the local ethnic and immigrant communities.

Affirmation, solidarity and critique - In Nieto's (2008) model evidence of this fifth level includes "two-way bilingual programs in which the languages of all students are used and maintained meaningfully in the academic setting" (p428) and "wherever possible, all students are learning to speak a second language" (p 429). Two-way bilingual programs, however, must necessarily begin in the early grades. For upper elementary, middle and high school, in addition to the expectation that all students learn to speak another language, this author suggests the added value of developing, re-capturing, sustaining, and retaining, the heritage languages of students. In instances where heritage language secondary programs thrive, instruction and curriculum for native and non-native speakers merge in the third or fourth year in Advanced Placement (AP) courses. At the AP level the backgrounds and skills of each stream of students are complimentary and mutually beneficial. Fortunately, teaching strategies and materials for both strands are doable within the general education program when supported by local attitudes and political will. While these shifts are no easy accomplishment, some schools are finding them achievable without either a Bilingual Education label, or a categorically funded program. Some districts in California (San Francisco Unified, Pasadena Unified, Ventura Unified School District) have adopted policies and administrative regulations that establish criteria for proficient bilingualism and acknowledge it by awarding a "Seal of Biliteracy" (CaliforniansTogether.org, 2010).

In addition, at this fifth level, this author would modify the "Children's Linguistic Human Rights" proposed by Tove Skutnabb-Kangas to the United Nations in 1989. to children and teachers who speak heritage languages of the community. In this adaptation, children as well as teachers, would have (1) the right to be positively identified with all the languages they speak and have these language(s) accepted and respected by others, (2) the right to use any, or all, of the talents and skills (including languages) in which they have competence for their own educational and/or psychological benefit or that of their students and (3) teachers would have the right to exercise professionally informed choices about when and how to use their talents and skills, including languages, in the instruction of their students, and finally (4) that non-bilingual teachers would share equally in the goals of student biliteracy through the use of strategies, materials and practices that engage and extend the students' reservoir of heritage language, whether or not the teacher has proficiency in that language, and whether or not there is a designated Bilingual Program.

The Adverse Social and Familial Impacts of Language Loss

Language loss, simply stated, is the attrition of language skills as a result of lack of use and aborted language development. Other kinds of skills, whether physical or intellectual, that go un-nurtured, can also be lost, unless the skill is so sufficiently well developed as to have been firmly internalized, such as riding a bicycle or playing a musical instrument.

It is no secret that generations of immigrants have traditionally been eager to assimilate and have historically urged their children to learn English as soon, and as well, as possible. This trajectory all too often results in well-intended immigrant parents and their children finding themselves without a shared meaningful language just a handful of years after entering the country. A desire to become fully American, which includes speaking English, and the social pressure to fit in--which includes not being different--has sometimes culminated in an unanticipated language gulf between parent and child in which neither party can communicate complex ideas in the language best understood by the other. Because of this, many children of immigrants are never able to carry on a dialogue with grandparents who do not speak English. They essentially do not get to really know their grandparents and never know what they have missed in the way of elderly wisdom, cultural values, and personal identity that derive from a sense of connectedness to family members and prior generations.

Benefits of Retaining Heritage Language

A recent meta-analysis (Adesope, Lavin, Thompson & Ungerleider, 2010) of the literature on cognitive benefits of bilingualism documents advantages accruing to bilinguals in "attentional control…working memory…metalinguistic awareness… metacognitive awareness…abstract or symbolic reasoning and creative and divergent thinking…[and] problem solving" (p 208-211). By virtue of their bilingualism, bilingual children know different words for the same object, thus understanding in the abstract that the object and the label are not one in the same. For example, "table" is understood as an object, but the label for the object of course varies from one language to another. Bilinguals score higher on standardized *tests of vocabulary*, from elementary through high school and even on the Graduate Record Exam (GRE), because of the ability for proficient bilinguals to draw on a greater reservoir of root words, prefixes, and suffixes to assist in deciphering otherwise unfamiliar vocabulary. On measures of *problem solving*, bilinguals demonstrate greater diversity in thinking, presumably due to diverse thinking strategies that accompany the variety of language structures they know and use. Enhanced *cultural insight* has also been credited to bilinguals, related again to the manner in which cultural perspectives are embedded in each language.

Language as a National Resource

In an era when the world grows smaller each day as a result of technological advances in travel and in communication, language is still a valued commodity that can help bridge services and products between countries and cultures with diverse languages. With a minimum of support, the wealth of language resources that exist by virtue of immigrant families could provide great political and cultural capital. Instead of immigrant languages being lost within a single generation, the U.S. could be a world leader in bilingualism. Heritage languages of immigrant families provide fertile ground for development of this natural resource. This is particularly true for adolescent and pre-adolescent immigrant students who arrive in U.S. schools with oral heritage language fluency commensurate with their chronological age, and heritage language literacy appropriate to their years of schooling in the heritage language. Many of these students have high levels of oral fluency in heritage languages making them a potential resource to our larger society and to our international relations.

Practical strategies for using Heritage Language in the Mainstream Classroom

- **Tapping the students' own stronger language for pre-writing brainstorming and for writing** can be an effective strategy with an adolescent newcomer who is literate, or can develop literacy, in the heritage language Preliminary writing in heritage language can be paraphrased, not translated – a much higher-level skill - into English to be submitted in English. To use this strategy effectively it is important to distinguish between an Adolescent Immigrant- English Learner (AI-EL) with some heritage language resources and a Long-Term - English Learner (LT-EL) whose former heritage language has been replaced by limited English. In the absence of a comprehensive heritage language history or assessment, a simple student survey can help make this distinction (see appendix).

- **Bridging between home and school with heritage language literature** is another strategy that has proven effective, especially with younger children. Children's books with a simple story line and pictures can be translated into either English or heritage language and read to a child by adults who speak each language at home or at school. Children's bilingual literature is ideal. An audio version of the story can be prepared in each language as well. Del Sol Books is an excellent source of Spanish/English/Bilingual Children's Books/CDs/DVDs, featuring *Alma Flor Ada*, F. Isabel Campoy, and Suni Paz.

- **Heritage language classes for native speakers,** discussed earlier in this chapter, are the hallmark of a school that has embraced the value of developing, recapturing, and sustaining heritage language while promoting global languages for native English speakers. "Spanish for Spanish Speakers" programs acknowledge that fluent Spanish speakers with little or no literacy have different needs from English speakers in beginning Spanish. By the third or fourth year, both groups come together in Spanish Literature and ultimately in Advanced Placement Spanish.

- **L-1 or L-2 Grouping practices** for cooperative of collaborative tasks or assignments can be varied by language or by English proficiency level, depending upon the specific learning objectives. For instance when the principle lesson objective is subject matter content or concepts, it can be very effective to group students by like-heritage language and mixed English proficiency levels. This grouping allows for student discussion to be bilingual – that is, in two languages. Students with the higher levels of bilingual proficiency typically emerge as the natural leaders of the group. Beginning and intermediate English Learners are benefitted by the academic use of heritage language, while at the same time being exposed to more advanced models of English proficiency spoken by same-language bilingual peers. For example, if the content is a laboratory Science, lab notes and labeled drawings can be done in whichever language is most dominant for each student and yet the final group assignment can be prepared and submitted in English. The fact that the language medium for the group process may have alternated back and forth between the two languages is a means to the end, rather than an end in itself. However, bi-products of this process are that both English Language Development (ELD) and heritage language retention (HLR) are supported while access to core curriculum is achieved. The teacher does not have to be bilingual in the language of the students to facilitate the bilingual learning environment.

- **L.O.T.E.** (language-other-than-English) **subject area textbooks** may be acquired from foreign Ministries of Education for student use – at home, in school, or in after school study groups ... with peers or with an adult. For example, the Ministry of Public Education (Ministerio de Educacion Publico) in Mexico regularly has a booth in the exhibitor section of state and national conferences for Bilingual Education (CABE, NABE) where they arrange to provide these materials, sometimes free of charge, to schools in the United States. Materials at designated grade levels, will of course, not necessarily correspond to the specific content standards of another country, but can be mined by the creative teacher for supplementary use by students either in the classroom or through the school library.

- **Universal (audio) access to written text** is available through a variety of instructional technology platforms– MacBooks, I-PAD, open source online curriculum – in which it is possible to convert text to speech by highlighting words, sentences or sections of text. This can serve as a read-along support for English Learners (EL) as well as struggling readers.

- **Preview as a means of creating prior knowledge.** All students benefit from some amount of prior knowledge when approaching new material. For English Learners (EL) this prior knowledge can be a form of preview done in the heritage language by means of aural or written translation, or aural or written paraphrasing. This can also be an effective means of establishing a context for culturally unfamiliar content, such as U.S. Government or U.S. History.

- **Chapter summaries for review** in heritage language. The same use of aural or written translation, or paraphrasing can also serve as a means to review content. By providing input in two languages, a learner with any amount of both languages will have experienced amplified content. Even highly proficient, bilingually balanced, educated adult immigrants who are well acculturated to the U.S. report studying both the English and the native language version of ballot initiatives in order to optimize their understanding of the issues or candidates in an elections. An important consideration in preparing heritage language translations or paraphrasing is that adolescent immigrants who may have been only partially schooled in the home country and in heritage language, may not have the academic literacy with which to benefit from the heritage language version at the same grade level as the English. This situation argues for using a sheltered English original from which to translate to heritage language, or a sheltered heritage language text.

- **Strategies and events to overcome linguistic discrimination.** Schools opting to embrace bilingualism as a policy will find that California Education code provides for awards in a variety of areas, one of which is biliteracy. A district may adopt policy and develop administrative regulations establishing criteria for the awarding of an official state of California "Seal of Biliteracy" for high school transcripts and diploma. (see appendix for sample policy developed by CaliforniansTogether.org).

  > "The Seal of Biliteracy is an award given by a school, school district or county office of education in recognition of students who have studied and attained proficiency in two or more languages by high school graduation. Appearing on the transcript of the graduating senior, the Seal of Biliteracy is a statement of accomplishment for future employers and for college admissions" (website: CaliforniansTogether.org.)

- The **Advanced Placement (AP) Exam** of the Educational Testing Service (ETS) is, of course a long established academic acknowledgement of language proficiency.

- **Transparency of essential information** provided in multiple languages, whether in audio and/or written form is the ultimate evidence of multicultural inclusion.

Examples include: safety rules, school immunization requirements, local and state graduation requirements, school attendance expectations and consequences, DMV rules of the road, and school grading systems. These represent information that students and their immigrant parents need to know long before they may be able to access the content either in oral or written form of English.

Questions for Discussion and Reflection

1. What are the heritage languages of students' families in your class, school, community?

2. In what informal and formal ways does - or could - your school, district, or community assure the positive status of heritage languages?

3. What teaching/learing strategies can you imagine using in your classroom that will engage students (and their parents') language strengths for academic purposes, even if you don't speak their languages?

4. What school-wide sanctioned awards and/or opportunities are there for students to use or develop their heritage language skills in academic and co-curricular activities?

5. To what extent is biliteracy valued in your school, district or community? Is a "seal of biliteracy" available for students who reach designated levels of multiple language proficiency?

Chapter 6

Transformative Education in Action Through the One Mind Group: How Recently Immigrated, Korean American Parents of Children with Special Needs Became Active Parent Advocates

by Eun Mi Cho

"It was like a spring shower of knowledge."

Mr. Han, parent,
after participating in an
LDA annual conference

Introduction

The Individuals with Disabilities Education Act Amendments of 1997 (IDEA) emphasized the rights of parents to participate in decisions about their children's education based on the belief that "strengthening the role of parents and ensuring that families of such children have meaningful opportunities to participate in the education of their children at school and at home" can improve the education of children with disabilities (Section 601(c) (5) (B). The purpose of this paper is to share a case study of how a group of Korean American parents and educators in the field of special education found a way to bridge the cultural and linguistic gaps in the "traditional school" for their children with special needs. This model demonstrates a working community group that can be replicated with other similar groups. The group's name, One Mind Group, can be translated into *Han Ma Eum Hwe* in Korean, which means, "helping each other as if we have One Mind." The members actively engaging in a transformative educational process demonstrate how recently immigrated Korean American parents of children with special needs can become active parent advocates in the United States.

Korean American Parents in the United States: Cultural Beliefs and Behaviors Related to Special Education

The U.S. Census Bureau (2000) projects that Asian Americans and Pacific Islanders (AAPI) will grow in number from approximately 9.5 million in 1997 to more than 35 million, or 9 percent of the U.S. population, by the year 2050. Among 10 million Asians in the United States, five groups numbered one million or more: Asian Indian, Chinese, Filipino, Korean, and Vietnamese. Together these groups make up about 80 percent of the Asian population with Chinese as the largest group followed by Filipino, Asian Indian, Vietnamese, and Korean (Census 2000 Special Reports, 2004). The AAPI group is one of the fastest growing minority groups in the United States and Korean Americans represent 1.1 million of this fast-growing population (U.S. Census Bureau, 2000). Therefore, the need for mainstream special education professionals to learn Korean culture seems especially salient to understand Korean American parents.

While Korean American parents' traditional way of thinking and living has taken on an important role of creating and maintaining strong Asian communities in America, some of the Korean cultural aspects may prevent easy integration with the mainstream culture (Cho, 1998). The primary traditional virtues that are still maintained in many of Korean American parents are filial piety, respect for elders, benevolence, loyalty, trust, cooperation, reciprocity, and humility (Hur & Hur, 1999). These traditional values are often challenged by the mainstream culture.

While Korean parents have a tendency to trust school administrators fully, mainstream administrators do not necessarily provide the full services for students without strong parental involvement. Many times the decisions of district administrators in special education depend more on allocated budget than that of each student's specific needs and benefits. Some behaviors or verbal remarks by Korean parents, from their modesty, may be taken by mainstream professionals as the sign of lack of interest in their children's education (Cho, 1998). Korean parents often say to teachers, "I don't know how to teach my kids at home," which implies "It's your job to educate my child with disabilities since you are the expert" even when they are very capable of teaching their children academics at home.

Recent immigrant Korean parents encounter serious complications when they attempt to understand and make sense of their child's disability within a mainstream cultural context. Some typical Korean perspectives toward disabilities from Korea hinder their being effective advocates for their children's special education. Typically,

Koreans believe supernatural influences cause disabilities and that belief leads them to feel helpless, depressed, or to blame themselves or their ancestors when they discover a disability in themselves or their family (Kim-Rupnow, 2001). Consequently, they seek little help and leave everything to fate. One popular old saying among Koreans goes, "Don't even look at the tree you can't climb," which depicts their belief very well. The child with a disability is often cared for by parents who usually expect and even believe that their child will outgrow such conditions. Unfortunately, these tendencies may cause the deficit of crucial intervention, which needs to begin as early as possible. The National Research Council (2002) asserts that early intervention wouldn't be possible without parents' involvement since it consists of the provision of services for both children with disabilities and their families, for the purpose of lessening the effects of the disabled condition. These programs usually are operated in home-based, center-based, hospital-based environments or a combination of these settings. Korean parents need to know that their child's disabling conditions may be overcome with appropriate medical intervention, and they may actively seek medicine, therapy, or surgery from health professionals. As explained by Korean Culture for Rehabilitation Service Providers, Kim-Rupnow (2001), Koreans use herbal medicines, acupuncture, and other natural remedies. In addition, being spiritually oriented, many Koreans using western medicine also offer prayers and conduct religious rituals to regain physical and mental health.

The difference in how cultures attend to the needs of their children further necessitates increasing the cultural competence, skills, and knowledge of the mainstream society when dealing with their child's disability issues. In a pilot study directed by this author (2004), the traditional Korean cultural-based virtues and attitudes of parents, especially toward their children with disabilities, have not changed significantly through mere residence in the United States, even when they may have been living here for longer than ten years. Park, Turnbull, & Park's (2001) research concurred with the author's pilot study. The research found that regardless of the parents' English proficiency, the length of time in the United States, involvement in American society, or education level, all of the parents seemed to keep Korean traditions and values to some extent and wanted professionals to take these cultural differences into account in working with them and their children. Here, then, are the discrepancies between two sets of cultural values regardless of length of residency in the U.S. in dealing with children with special needs.

Korean American parents are a major force in their children's development and success in life, often involving discipline and dedication (*Handbook for Teaching Korean-American Students*, 1992). However, when it comes to the education of children with disabilities, unique aspects of Korean culture come into play and affect the attitudes of Korean American parents. For example, they are not familiar with the mainstream American concepts of empowerment and parity between teachers and parents, so they tend to believe that special education professionals are generally the decision makers for their children with disabilities (Cho, 1998). Empowerment as described by Kalyanpur and Rao (1999) refers to "changing the role of a service provider from that of an expert to that of an ally or friend who enables families to articulate what they need" (National Center for the Dissemination of Disability Research). This is inconsistent with Korean American parents and their value system. It might not be easy to think of their child's teacher as their partner because most Korean American parents utilize a hierarchal relationship in interpersonal communication based on age, social status, and education (Cho, 1998). Parents consider teachers to be higher on the hierarchy. Turnbull and Turnbull (2001) portrayed American empowered parents as "... assertive, knowledgeable, and empowered and fighting against..." in the school system to attain their children's rights; whereas, Korean American parents are more modest in their expression and tend to show respect toward special education professionals (p.30).

One Mind Group Members' Cultural Attitudes before Transformative Education

One Mind Group is a Korean American Parents Support Group for children with disabilities. Some of the common problems that are easily exhibited among One Mind Group members before undertaking a transformative change due to Korean cultural aspects are as follows.

First, the over-submissive attitude of One Mind Group Korean American parents toward special education professionals has been a problem in their getting appropriate special education and related services for their children. Without understanding the fact that Korean American parents' over-compliant attitudes come from respect toward professionals as authority figures, mainstream American special education professionals may overlook the parents' modesty. Most Korean American parents who came to the support group as new members shared that they usually tried to follow teachers' suggestions at IEP meetings and conferences, regardless of their level of acculturation. They rarely disagreed with professional's opinions, nor did they challenge their authority by posing questions, even if they privately had other opinions.

Conversational style differences between professionals and Korean American parents also played a critical role. In a study by Park, Turnbull, & Park (2001), a Korean American parent noted, "As you also know, we Koreans are very compliant to professionals, especially teachers. We are taught to say `yes' to teachers; whereas, being assertive is so important in this country." The researchers also agreed, "Traditionally, Korean culture emphasizes deference and compliance with professionals, including teachers. Therefore, the parents may appear passive or uninterested. These parents, however, may be very dedicated to their children's achievement."

The following paragraph from the *Handbook for Teaching Korean-American Students* helps mainstream educators understand Korean American parents' attitudes.

> Korean-American parents fully depend on teachers for the teachers' wisdom and expertise. Therefore, most of them believe that their role is to respect, listen, and follow the professional judgment of teachers and administrators. Most Korean-American parents consider it their responsibility to assist the school by deferring to the authority of teachers and administrators. (1992, p. 47)

It is likely that Korean American parents will passively follow the directions of their children's teachers and administrators in most cases; whereas, mainstream American parents actively advocate for their rights during Individualized Education Program (IEP) meetings. A parents' role as equal members at the IEP meetings is a key factor to getting the necessary special education and related services for their children with special needs in the U.S.

Second, collectivism has a direct effect on Korean people's lives (Gudykunst, Matsumoto, Ting-Toomey, Nishica, Kim, & Heyman, 1996). Members of the One Mind Group practice the beliefs initiated by the hierarchy in their lives. The collectivistic cultures learn the major values, such as harmony and solidarity, and the members also acquire preferred ways to conceive of themselves consistent with that culture. While the mainstream Americans' emphasis is on individualism, Korean Americans emphasize harmony with order, which leads them to be influenced by the opinions of other members of their family or community when making decisions (Kim-Rupnow, 2001).

Korean Americans think that any family member is part of their family group; therefore, they remain strongly connected with one another in extended family systems. Consequently, having a child with disabilities means an embarrassment not only for the child's nuclear family, but also for the child's extended family. Korean American siblings show low self-esteem if they have a disabled sibling, especially when they are in the process of getting married (Cho, 1994). Parents and relatives of the bride or groom to be have a difficult time deciding whether to let the marriage happen or not if they know that they are going to add a person to their family with disabilities. As a consequence, most Korean American parents of children with disabilities have a common tendency not to expose their children to society.

Third, a negative view of disability within Korean culture comes from a lack of knowledge about the various types of disabilities. Kim-Rupnow (2001) asserts,

> It is common for Koreans to embrace a complex mixture of beliefs regarding the causes and treatments of a disability, depending mainly on their education, religion, and family background....Some Koreans believe that lifelong disability is a kind of payback for something they did wrong in the past. As a result, many Koreans with disabilities and their families suffer from shame, helplessness, denial, withdrawal and depression. Many view the acquired disability as the result of bad luck or misfortune.

The knowledge and understanding of Korean American parents of special education and related services are constrained by their own upbringing in a culture that has offered minimal special education services. Some Korean American parents think of a specific learning disability as mental retardation (Cho, 1994). Other Korean American parents think that their children will outgrow their specific learning disabilities even though a specific learning disability is not curable; but, it is a life-long disability.

Educating for Understanding

Before the training began with the One Mind Group, members did not have a scientific understanding of their child's disabilities. Parents need education with scientific research-based information to help them understand that disabling conditions may be overcome or reduced with appropriate medical intervention, active therapies, and/or even some surgeries. Because of these problems, it is very important that Korean American parents learn to communicate effectively with the mainstream American special education professional to obtain the correct information about their child's disabilities and to participate in necessary workshops and conferences.

Although the Individuals with Disabilities Education Act (1997) and the No Child Left Behind Act (2002) assure active involvement of parents for their children's education, most One Mind Group members did not take active roles in the decision making process for their children with disabilities. Based on qualitative research done by

Park, Turnbull, and Park (2001), Korean American parents regarded special education rights, such as free public education or free transportation, as "blessings" rather than "rights." Parents hesitated to raise questions or disagree with the agencies, question the performance of professionals, or request assistance related to their rights. Knowing their parental rights was the first step to taking an active role.

Beyond the Theoretical and into Practical Applications through One Mind Group

With the growing need for organizing a support group for Korean-speaking parents of children with disabilities, a number of parents, along with the author, organized a group called One Mind Group in 1998. Its purpose was to act in support of Korean American parents of children with special needs and their other family members. The area of support has been expanded to the Northern part of California, but the main focus was within the greater Sacramento area.

Coordinating Procedure: On the 4th of April 1998, the Learning Disabilities Association (LDA), Sacramento Affiliate held a Special Education Parent and Professional Training Seminar in Sacramento sponsored by Area Board III, a federally funded state agency for people who have developmental delays. The author, a Korean American bilingual special education teacher and multicultural committee chair of LDA, Sacramento at that time, invited Korean-speaking parents of children with disabilities to the training seminar. She translated the main content of the seminar into Korean in print and disseminated the information to fifteen Korean American families with children with disabilities through personal contacts and provided the printed information to thirty-two Korean American churches in the greater Sacramento area. Korean American churches are the most comfortable places for many Korean American parents to expose their children with disabilities (Cho, 1994). In addition, to reaching out to more Korean Americans who might have interests in learning about special education, the author sent the same information to two Korean American daily newspapers and five Korean grocery stores where such information might be shared with others in the local Korean American community.

During the seminar, the author simultaneously interpreted the content of the seminar for the Korean-speaking audience. Twenty-two Korean American participants expressed their excitement with learning parents' rights and responsibilities related to their children's special education and related services. Immediately after the training, the author suggested having a discussion meeting about what she and the other Korean American participants learned from the seminar. She also explained the importance of having a support group for Korean speaking parents to be effective advocates for their children with disabilities. Then, with the strong commitment among participants, she was able to coordinate a support group. Those twenty-two Korean-speaking participants in that training seminar included parents, pastors, social workers, adults with disabilities, and a special education teacher. An election for officers followed along with the naming of the group as One Mind Group. Ever since the initial meeting, the members of One Mind Group have been meeting monthly or bi-monthly, on the third Saturday of the month.

Membership: One Mind Group is composed of the following membership: Korean American parents of individuals with exceptional needs who attend public or private schools in the greater Sacramento area; Korean American individuals with exceptional needs; Korean American professionals who work in the field of human development; representatives of other agencies concerned with individuals with special needs; and other interested persons.

There have been various formal trainings, discussion group meetings, family picnics, one-on-one conferences, participation in professional conferences and workshops, special parties for children with disabilities, and special events for siblings without disabilities. Other events include summer camping trips, and sharing sessions about IEP meetings and other informal learning about different disabilities and relevant resources among group members.

Seminars by guest speakers are continuing with the following topics: (1) how to deal with the stresses and anxieties in raising children with special needs and how to maintain quality relationships among family members, especially between a husband and a wife by Korean-speaking psychologists; (2) how to prepare for IEP meetings, due process, and how to read assessment results by Korean American special education teachers; (3) how to utilize social services related to disabilities by Korean American social workers. Additionally, to help members understand specific learning disabilities, the group participated in a learning disability simulation. They experienced temporarily having specific learning disabilities by using a learning disabilities simulation kit. Discussion group meetings occur regularly. The author and members bring articles about different topics related to disabilities; they then form groups to read and to share their reflections on their reading. The author also holds one-on-one conferences for each member of the group with help for his or her individual problems as needed. Parents have been participating in professional conferences held by various organizations, such as CalTASH (The Association for Persons with Severe Handicaps in 1983; Equity, Diversity,

Social Justice and Inclusion in 2005), MIND (Medical Investigation of Neurological Disorders) Institute, and LDA (Learning Disabilities Association).

Individual Educational Plan (IEP) sharing sessions are one of the key activities of the group. Parents bring their children's IEP documents to check with the author and to go over them with other members dealing with similar disabilities. All members take turns sharing their experiences of their IEP meetings. Members get new ideas by listening to each other's experiences and by participating in other family's IEP meetings. The support group has presented an overview of special education agencies, programs, and services including: special education laws, legislative affairs, and infant and preschool programs. Other areas covered are in the area of evaluation and assessment, free and appropriate education, least restrictive environments and placement, related services-interagency responsibilities, the individual education plan process, advocacy, and due process.

The above activities take place during the support group's monthly meetings. Each member takes a turn to open his or her house to host meetings. Each family brings food to share with other members. Members bring their children with special needs to the meetings. Adults or young adults with disabilities have also been participating. The meetings have been a positive experience for members in both social/supportive and educational/advocacy aspects. While parents take educational training and participate in small group discussions at each meeting, their children with disabilities and their siblings without disabilities become engaged with educational play in a separate room under the supervision of Korean American youth group members from either a local Korean church or a High School Asian Student Association. Through the volunteer work, some of the youth helpers discovered a passion for studying in the field of special education at the college level.

The One Mind Group members have been able to transform their attitudes toward disabilities within the three major Korean cultural perspectives ever since the first meeting in 1998. Those three areas of Korean American parents' cultural aspects which have direct impact on their children's special education were: overly submissive attitudes toward special education professionals, lack of knowledge about their rights and different disabilities, and a collectivistic mindset that is foreign to mainstream American special educators. Members indicated that their broadened capability enhanced their ability to reach beyond the point of their expectations.

The transformative educational process described in this article was a pedagogy that helped Korean American parents to be knowledgeable of their rights primarily and then guided them to practice those rights in their community and at their children's schools for their children with special needs. Through the process of education and application, parents were able to transform their views of their own identity. Before the transformative education through One Mind Group activities, they believed that they were the ones who brought the societal problems to the community by giving birth to defective children. The educational opportunities and experiential activities from the One Mind Group have changed the members' beliefs and attitudes to the degree that they can share their expertise as parents of children with special needs and raise their children successfully to become competent citizens for the community.

Transformative Changes Through the One Mind Group	
Before	**After**
1. They rarely disagreed with professional's opinions or challenged their authority by posing questions even if they privately had other opinions. They used to believe that special education professionals were the decision makers for their children with disabilities.	1. They began to believe in their own capabilities with self-efficacy in mind.

	2. They are knowledgeable about their children's disabilities and the special education service delivery systems.
	  • One Mind Group members became parent resource specialists for other parents.
	  • The negative aspects of Korean traditional beliefs toward disabilities have less control over them.

2. Some Korean American parents think of a specific learning disability as mental retardation.	

3. Members did not have a scientific understanding of their child's disabilities.	3. They are competent to attain the appropriate special education and related services for their children's special needs.
	  • They know how to put forth a sustained effort and how to handle their roles as parent-advocates.
	  • Members achieved a clearer understanding of the special education system and related laws and policies.

4. One Mind Group members did not take active roles in the decision making process for their children with disabilities.	
	4. Members now feel more comfortable taking partner roles with mainstream American special education professionals at schools and in the IEP (Individualized Education Program) process.

One Mind Group now has a growing membership, both locally and in other parts of the state. Its model serves as an example for other communities in the region.

Systematic Parents Helping Parents: Some members of the group who are highly educated and acculturated to mainstream American culture are less limited in their English proficiency. They are comfortable with mainstream values and social relationships, and most are bilingual. These members may be individuals who were born in Korea, but were raised in this country and have lived in the U.S. most of their lives, or they were born and raised in this country of Korean American parents. They participate in other Korean-only speaking members' IEP meetings to offer support. Since limited English proficiency was the biggest barrier for many of the members in the process, they developed a system of "Parents Helping Parents."

One thing that has been successfully implemented is composing sub-groups in the group based on the children's school districts. For example, parents of children who attend schools in the same school district are responsible to each other to participate in IEP meetings for their children with disabilities. Some parents have English fluency while others are less fluent. They usually meet before the IEP meeting to go over the agenda that the parents developed for the child. Those without enough information on the content of their children's IEP meetings or a clear understanding about their rights as parents gain tremendous benefit from the IEP preparation meetings with other bilingual parents. Connecting experienced members with new members whose children have just been diagnosed with disabilities has been useful.

Future Plan: One Mind Group will continue its transformative education in the group to empower each other while the members expand the educational opportunities to the Korean American community to transform public perspectives regarding disability issues. Since they learned how to access the necessary information on different websites, not only will they utilize them for their own empowerment, but they will also enhance their use of the vast information available to transform the Korean American community. The development of a parent handbook, *Things to Know When your Child is Diagnosed with Disabilities* and the steps on "How to Get the Right Education and Services for your Child with Disabilities" is another publication the group has distributed. They know that many federally funded parent information, training centers, and an information packet in both English and Korean are available on the web. They will continue not only to build stronger connections as a group to help each other, but also to educate themselves with new special education and services. They are not going to participate in any IEP meeting without understanding the required IEP content and components and parental right to sign the important documents. Their advocacy skills include representing and seeking necessary help for their children's needs. Their goal in advocating for their children's rights is the beginning of an equal partnership with mainstream American special education educators and professionals.

Although it has been common practice that mothers seem to take charge of the children's education in Korean families (Kim, 1996), as time has passed, stronger involvement of fathers has been the case in the One Mind Group. The fathers provide very important aspects of information regarding parenting practices. In the Korean family structure, the father is the primary decision maker as the family representative and principal provider (Chan, 1998). The members will continue to involve fathers in the group function.

Helpful Suggestions When Working with Korean American parents

1. Mainstream American special education professionals need to build positive and collaborative relationships with Korean American parents regardless of their child's age or type of disability. The following are some ways to begin building relationships:
   - Be aware of communication style differences. Many Korean parents believe and practice the old saying, "Silence is Golden" in their communication while special education professionals believe that "the squeaky wheel gets the oil."
   - Be patient for ongoing communication. Keep in mind that most Korean parents have practiced "waiting for their turn to talk during conversation."
   - Try to use a few basic Korean greetings to build rapport in the initial stage.
   - Do home visits. Most Korean parents take home visits by their child's teachers as an honor. Parents will provide valuable information to you, such as the Korean ways of raising children with disabilities at home and in their community.
   - Use various ways of communication with Korean parents. Add written information to verbal communication whenever possible since most Korean Americans' reading and writing skills are better than their conversational skills. Even in their conversations, receptive language fluency is much better than expressive.
   - Develop and use the list of Korean American cultural brokers and/or cultural centers for important meetings with Korean parents, such as Student Study Team meetings, IEP meetings, and parent-teacher conferences. Korean Americans consider the opinions of important community members rather highly.
   - Make sure Korean American parents know about their parental rights. Most

Korean Americans are not accustomed to the idea of "parents having rights in the school structure." They believe the hierarchical social relationship which puts the status of teachers is higher than that of parents.
- Ask Korean American parents questions respectfully whenever you don't understand their traditional rituals and customs.

1. Korean American parent voice: The following is a list of some of the main characteristics of mainstream American special education professionals who were the most helpful or least helpful during the journey of getting services from them (Data from the interviews with One Mind Group members):

   a. The most helpful characteristics of professionals
      - Professional and competent about special education and disabilities as an expert.
      - Passionate toward their work and caring for children and their parents. Make phone calls to inform the student's progress and visit home to get connected.
      - Respectful to parents and cultural differences by trying to learn Korean greetings and some of cultural practices.
      - Share the same goal of providing the best education for children.
      - Focus on students' potential and abilities, rather than disabilities.

   b. The least helpful characteristics of professionals
      - Insensitivity to parents' English fluency level or lack of care to maintain communication between teachers and parents. Send important notes home written in English regardless of parents' English fluency. No phone calls to follow up.
      - Low expectation of students' performance.
   - Treat students unfairly.
      - Unreliable. Do not follow through on their promises. Do not keep appointments with parents without giving parents timely notice.

Questions for Reflection and Discussion:

1. Reflecting on the suggestions above, what plan can you develop to work with students from Korean cultures?

2. Reflecting on the suggestions above, how will you handle the situation when Korean American parents are hesitant to raise questions, disagree with IEP team members, or request assistance related to their rights?

3. Using a graphic organizer or Venn diagram demonstrate how Korean American parent groups are similar or differ from other cultural groups that are not part of the mainstream culture.

The author focused more on recently immigrated, Korean-American parents in this article rather than those who were been born and raised in the U.S. as second or third generation Korean Americans.

Chapter 7

Empowered Parents Transform School Districts: Fighting for Bilingual Programs

by Olivia M. Gallardo

*To create the changes needed, however, is not only a matter of
professional development—it is also a matter of whether or not our
schools, state and nation have the will to provide what's needed, and
the courage and commitment to reckon with the deep-seated patterns of
excluding certain groups of children - especially children of color, poor
children and language minority children.*

Laurie Olson and Ann Jaramillo
Turning the Tides of Exclusion (1999, p.23)

Schools Mandate English-Only Programs

On June 2, 1998 California's English learners experienced a major change in the
schools that continues to affect children across the country. Anti-immigrant bias, along
with little understanding on how bilingual education programs work, brought about the
approval of a law that purported to end bilingual programs in the schools. Crawford's
(2000, p. 10) analysis as to the one-sided 61-39 percent victory of Proposition 227
indicates that by exploiting a set of fears and beliefs felt by the majority of the electorate,
the media were able to manipulate information reporting that cultivated controversy.
Crawford states:

> By nature, journalism must simplify subject matter to make it meaningful
> to a wide audience. Often this means highlighting the sharpest points of
> conflict – in this case, language of instruction....So it is likely that voters
> paid little heed to factors such as students' poverty and lack of access to
> reading materials, the shortage of trained teachers, and various resource
> constraints. (p.10)

Proposition 227 went into effect, changing overnight the way children were taught English in schools throughout the state of California. Thirty years of research on how children learn their second language at a level competitive to English-only children had no bearing on the votes. Studies by Hakuta, (2000), Thomas and Collier (1997), Krashen, Crawford, and Kim (1998) address English learners' performance concluding that students perform best when given four to six years of native-language instruction in developmental programs or two-way immersion programs. None of the research mattered and California school administrators and resource staff proceeded to put a program into place that provided sheltered English immersion classes for 1.4 million English learners (California Department of Education, 1998).

Defining Sheltered English Immersion: What It Is Not

The summer of 1998 began with school districts scrambling to put together a sheltered immersion program as mandated by Proposition 227. California Education Code, Education Code Section 305, (1999) states:

> English learners shall be educated through sheltered English immersion during a temporary transition period not normally to exceed one year. Local schools shall be permitted to place in the same classroom English learners of different ages but whose degree of English proficiency is similar....Once English learners have acquired a good working knowledge of English, they shall be transferred to English language mainstream classrooms.

Educators and other practitioners in the field of second language acquisition had never practiced "sheltered immersion" or for that matter heard of such a program. Sheltered English is a term familiar to teachers, but sheltered immersion as defined did not have any theoretical basis or practice. Sheltered English and sheltered immersion are two completely different concepts.

To better understand the issues raised by Proposition 227, an understanding of sheltered English, also known as Specially Designed Academic Instruction in English (SDAIE) needs further explanation. SDAIE refers to a methodology supported by research and practitioners in the field of English language development. This approach includes grade-level course objective designs and content-comprehensible material for English language learners. It provides additional support to English learners, rather than leaving them to "sink or swim" in a content class designed for native English-speakers (Echevarria, Vogt, & Short, 2004).

Students who speak English at an intermediate fluent level--meaning that these students have at least two years of English language development-- can progress to a sheltered English classroom environment. These individuals understand and speak English; however, the students need more time before they can function in a mainstream classroom at the same level as a native speaker. Sheltered English helps the student improve his or her reading and writing ability. After a year of sheltered English, students are tested using specific criteria. If they can pass the speaking, reading, and writing portions of the test, they are redesignated and transferred to a mainstream classroom. In California, the California English Language Development Test (CELDT) is used for testing students on their English ability and progress.

Sheltered English immersion, on the other hand, does not have a body of scientific research to support it. It is defined as an English language acquisition process for young children for whom nearly all classroom instruction is in English, but with the curriculum and presentation designed for children who are learning the language (California Department of Education, 1999). Methodology for sheltered immersion may be confused with immersion programs that have proven successful in the United States and other countries. There are numerous studies using an "immersion program" design, which has as its goal complete fluency in two languages. Canadian-based programs using French immersion strategies started in St. Lambert, Montreal, in 1965. Middle-class parents persuaded school district administrators to set up an experimental kindergarten class of twenty-six children. The aim was for students to become bilingual without loss of academic achievement. The St. Lambert experiment succeeded, influencing bilingual education in Europe and other countries. These immersion programs are similar to those used in the United States and referred to as dual language programs or two-way development programs. There are over one thousand research studies using immersion programs, and all aim to develop fully bilingual children (Baker, 1997).

In California and other states, dual language immersion programs have emerged as most successful in teaching and learning a second language. The emphasis is on learning a second language for both groups in the program. English-dominant and target-language-dominant students are purposefully integrated with the goal of developing bilingual skills, academic excellence, and positive cross-cultural and personal competency attitudes for both groups of students (Lindholm-Leary, 2001). Sheltered English immersion has none of the strategies or methodologies mentioned. It aims to teach English in English.

Complying with Proposition 227

The passage of Proposition 227 created immediate challenges for school districts. Curriculum specialists, given the job to put together the new programs, worked all summer preparing a set of frequently-asked questions and answers (FAQ's) that teachers and staff would need when beginning the school year.

Many districts, given the opportunity, changed their programs without hesitation, announcing to their staff that they no longer provided bilingual education, and classroom instruction would follow the state guidelines, which meant sheltered English immersion classrooms became the norm for the English language learner. Other districts fought for the rights of their students, taking every advantage of the law to continue their bilingual programs under the alternative or other programs. Under section 310 of the law, a parent or legal guardian could receive a waiver if the individual personally visited the school and applied for it:

> Parents may request a waiver from the structured English immersion process for their children to be taught English and other subjects through bilingual education or other recognized educational methods. Before entering an alternative program, children must be in English-Language classrooms for 30 days. (Education Code sections 310-311 and California Code of Regulations, Title 5 Section 11303)

School districts fighting for their students' rights applied for special program rights and overall restructured their programs adding dual immersion or two-way immersion programs. Chaos reigned in many districts of the state. One school in particular that the author remembers visiting had collected all the Spanish reading books from the classrooms. Books and other materials were stored in the cafeteria with instructions to throw away all materials written in another language. Other districts neglected to mention the waiver process to parents, and the fact that alternate programs existed. Several years later teachers still were not sure what was myth and what was law.

One school district in particular elected to change its policy on bilingual education and concentrate its efforts on implementing sheltered immersion programs. A parent group courageously took a stance against the schools' policies, successfully overturning the school board and superintendent's position on alternative program design. This is their story.

District Implements Sheltered Instruction

With the opening of the new school year in the fall of 1998, the school district sent home an improperly-worded memo in Spanish stating that English will be taught in *"su idioma,"* which means "their language." Parents read this and thought they didn't need a waiver for English immersion classes because children were going to be taught in their primary language (*Ledger Dispatch*, 1998). Consequently, at the beginning of the school year, the district received six requests to remain in bilingual classrooms out of 1,300 limited English-speaking students.

Teachers returned to their classrooms with no other choice but to follow their schools' mandates. Classrooms would no longer have materials in Spanish. Books, wall posters, charts and letters of the alphabet were all in English. The author spoke to one of the teachers who had become a close acquaintance over the years, asking her what happened to all her Spanish material. She reported that the district would no longer offer bilingual programs and those teachers formerly serving bilingual students would now be in sheltered settings. Furthermore, if they did not follow school procedures, they would be transferred.

School started smoothly with the major difference that children in all grades including kindergarten were now spoken to in English. As the weeks went by, children began to complain to their parents that they did not understand the teacher. Over a summer, a highly successful bilingual school providing a program that encouraged children to learn two languages and transitioned children into all English classrooms by fourth grade, ended its bilingual program. Parents for the most part did not notice or question the new policies. However, one group of parents began to dispute the implementation of the new law. They filled the board meetings asking questions and seeking answers about the lack of information for waivers and their children's right to an alternative program.

One of the community members shared that other issues began to emerge, "Comments were coming from children's teachers, including bus drivers, that bilingual students speak only English. This problem seriously hindered the student's self esteem."

Parents and Community Fight Back

The parents were angry, frustrated, and feeling helpless, so they decided to examine the new law more closely, investigate their legal rights, and unite. One of the parents stated, "What the district personnel were not aware of was that the Spanish-speaking parents were very *"Trucha"* (meaning alert).

Parents began to question their school principals. The principals could only point to the policies of the district and reiterate that the law stated children were to learn in English. At one elementary school, the district's superintendent addressed the parents. He stated that the bilingual programs no longer existed, that the law (227) would be implemented and that the students would be placed in a total immersion program. From an administrative perspective, that was the end of the discussion.

A Checklist of <u>Historical Events Leading to Parental Empowerment</u>

- Recognition that the district was not seriously addressing the issues of their children, the parents and some bilingual teachers started to meet at the local church. Discussion centered on what was going on district-wide. They were recognizing the lack of concern by school administrators and their inability to communicate with school sites.
- Bilingual teachers and church officials working collaboratively let parents know of the next meeting at a local park.
- Parents and important educators met at a local park, inviting a well-known political activist from Los Medanos Community College, bilingual teachers, and other community members.
- The public meeting discussed the following issues:

    1. Information on educational programs for bilingual students.
    2. Common *"mal"* or bad treatment of bilingual children.
    3. The need to develop a plan to address these political issues.

The participating parents were well-educated and they clearly articulated their concerns. The plan developed and included the following:

- Invite a representative from the Office of Civil Rights.
- The issues discussed would be centered on a violation of civil rights (Lau Issues) focusing on the premise of "equal access to education."

Frustrated by the lack of response at the board meetings, and at the affected schools, informed groups found many ways of gathering key persons to plan and evaluate how Proposition 227 could work for them. At one meeting the author attended the group included the former language specialist of the school district, a group of teachers who did not agree with the new school policies, two university professors, and a small group of parents. The informal meeting helped all individuals by putting into perspective the issues affecting their schools. The following concerns were discussed:

- Parents were not sufficiently informed of the new program and the waiver policy.
- School district personnel and board members were not listening to the parents' grievances.
- Teachers felt intimidated and uninformed.
- Parents noticed that their children's' work was below standard because they did not understand the teachers.

The meeting proved to be one of the important vehicles to help parents reach out and inform other parents. This event and others like it would transform the whole school district and prepare parents to take on jobs they never imagined themselves capable of doing. In her work with parents in Carpinteria, Delgado-Gaitan (1991) observed that when given the opportunity, parents take on roles that are empowering and bring about change for themselves and their community. Delgado-Gaitan (1991) emphasizes a difference between a conventional model of parent involvement, which she feels represents a domination of power on the part of the district and their attempt to make the family conform to the school and a non-conventional model. In the non-conventional model (see Table 7.1), parents play an active role in their child's education with the goal of maximizing their learning as well as their children's.

What transpired at the community meeting the author attended followed the non-conventional model of involvement. Each group at this initial meeting took on a responsibility. One group concentrated its efforts on informing the parents of their children's rights and the waiver process. The parent group felt that it needed help attracting other parents. It lacked the experience of bringing together a large group. A plan was put into place with the intent of educating parents on the importance of the mother tongue and its relation to learning English. This would help parents understand the importance of bilingual programs. The objective was to increase a parent's understanding of the language-learning process and how it tied into the services and programs their children needed to learn English. By having informed parents, the group felt it would be easier to ask for their support at the school board meetings. Two

Table 7.1
Non-Conventional Model
Parent Involvement for Empowerment

Purpose of parent involvement	To learn the school system through information meetings which teach school laws, rules, and responsibilities.
Recognition of parents' importance and their role	Parents acknowledge that a lack of information exists and commit themselves to learn.
What we want to accomplish	Develop an awareness of what constitutes parent involvement and its role in the school environment. Build programs for interested parents who learn from each other while diminishing their feelings of powerlessness and isolation. Admit that there is a need for developing their skills and participating in their children's schooling.
Develop leadership skills	Parents are invited to attend parent conferences and meetings that teach leadership skills. Leadership workshops are developed based on appropriate educational level of attendees.
Establish collective critical reflection	Meetings are hands-on with on-going dialogue between presenters and parents. Sharing common experiences prepares them to take collective action.
Confront stereotypes	• Parents are interested in child's education. • Primary language and limited formal education do not lessen ability and interest to participate. • Long working hours are acknowledged but not an excuse for not participating.

Source: Delgado-Gaitan, C. (1991)

professors from the local university attending the planning meeting were asked to provide the parents an in-service on how the first language supports a stronger academic second language. The group was ready to go to work.

Another group planned on preparing well-written, clear statements to be presented at the school board meetings: They would present the board with their grievances and concerns in giving their children an education that by law included what is known as an alternate program. This alternate program can be designed as a bilingual program. Parents began their fight with little knowledge but each meeting increased their knowledge.

In the past, the typical pattern has been that the more socially powerful group has devalued the identities of the less powerful group and rationalized this as being in the group's best interest. Under these conditions subordinated group members often partially internalize the ways they are defined or positioned by the dominant group and come to see themselves as inferior (Cummins, 1996, p.12). This point became evident in the group as group members gave a reason why they could not undertake the task at hand. However, in teams, they moved forward to their respective assigned tasks determined to change the present policy.

The Struggle Begins

Parents planning the school in-service feared that only a small group would attend. The professors worked with the parent team showing them how to write the flyers. They added an incentive coupon to the flyer for prizes such as books and pencils. Flyers were neon bright and personally distributed by the parents. They stood outside of the school mornings and afternoons distributing the bright neon announcements. One of the educators working with this committee determined that teachers would be a good source to provide names of parents who could help spread word of the meeting. Each teacher contacted said "no." They could not help because they believed it would jeopardize their teaching positions. It took much coaxing and trust-building for those teachers to begrudgingly provide some parent names for the committee.

The day arrived for the in-service. It was 6:00 p.m. and only a few rows in the front were occupied. The in-service started. Krashen's theory on comprehensible input splashed across the screen on easy-to-read transparencies in Spanish. It was 6:15 and half of the seats were now filled. Cummins' theories on surface fluency and academic language followed with examples and a lot of discussion. By 6:30 the whole cafeteria was filled to capacity. Parents sat glued to their seats asking question after question. Finally, the session moved to an explanation of Proposition 227 and the needed waivers. One of the professors explained what waivers were, and a parent asked the principal whether the waivers were available to sign. The few parents who had planned the meeting beamed at the outcome. Fallacies of the parents' ability to understand theories and methodology were breaking down with each hour of the meeting.

School Board Confrontation

The group of parents planning the school board presentations did not have an easy job. Each meeting the parents and brave teachers filled the meeting rooms but without results. Parents had limited time to present their grievances. Board members did not seem to know the law as well as the parents, and they continued to assert that bilingual programs no longer existed in their school district. Parents did not give up. They continued on to Sacramento filing complaints with the state Board of Education and the state Office of Civil Rights. An investigation of the school district followed with findings supporting the parents' grievances. The district was not meeting the children's educational needs.

Needless to say, five years later, this district has undergone many changes. One of the parents at that first meeting ran for the district Board of Education and won. The superintendent was unable to hold his job, and a new superintendent that supports bilingual education and two-way immersion programs took his place. A forceful and dynamic contingent of parents continued its trips to Sacramento. They became part of the planning group writing a law that went into effect, which now supports all parents in the state.

Reflection

This story demonstrates how parents, when respected and informed, can be advocates for teachers and their children. Bilingual education programs need strong parent partnerships and an informed administration to work at their finest. Proposition 227 won, but educators and parents used this law to improve programs and change what was not working before.

Political leaders and educators in the community outlined some of the emerging issues:

- Recognition that issues were political and not educational.
- The treatment of bilingual children affected their learning.
- Parents were recognizing the loss of their children's dignity.
- Teachers in the former bilingual program also felt disrespected.
- District-wide there was a lot of resentment toward the superintendent. For years following the Proposition 227 fight, many effective teachers and supportive administrators left the district. One of these administrators was the director of the bilingual program.

Community members and parents also had positive experiences that continue to help the community grow:

- The Spanish-speaking community realized that its unity and belief in bilingual education led to the changes in its school district.
- The older generation had the knowledge and was supported by the younger generation; both worked together to change events.
- There was recognition of the value of multiculturalism and the importance of all ethnicities having the right to their culture. Latino, Sicilians, Italians, African-Americans, Filipinos, Greeks, and others are all part of this community.

Demographic changes will continue. Immigration, legal or undocumented, will bring new languages and new ethnicities to this country; consequently, a knowledgeable citizenship should not sit back as other conservative groups find ways to move toward a "melting pot theory," again. Crawford (2000, p. 123) raises painful but inescapable questions for bilingual educators throughout the United States. These questions are included for reflection and discussion. I would like to thank Board Member Ruben Rosales and Dr. Angel Valencia for their contributions to this chapter.

Questions for Discussion and Reflection

I. Thinking about the passage of Proposition 227 and other similar laws in other states, reflect and discuss the following questions.

1. How long can an unpopular pedagogy be sustained--especially one that depends on public funding and, in some cases, legal mandates for survival?

2. Why are the opponents of bilingual education expanding their influence over voters and policymakers?

3. What strategies offer hope for changing people's minds about the program before it is dismantled or restricted?

4. Who will take the lead in organizing to defend bilingual education?

II. How does your school support parent participation?

1. Make a chart showing the various events your school sponsors for parents.

2. How do these meetings or events help parents to become leaders in the school and their community?

By Myself
by Stephen Fisher

When I am by myself
And I close my eyes
I'm thinking of all the great memories I have
I'm with my family
I'm on a farm in the small town of Albion
I'm an hour away from the nearest Wal-Mart or McDonalds
I'm helping Dad feed the cattle and pigs
I'm playing with my older brothers
I'm eating the afternoon snack Mom would cook us
I'm in school with my friends
I'm fishing at the lake relaxing
I'm watching Husker games on Saturdays with friends
I'm playing with our dog Odie
I'm riding our horse Mickey
I'm enjoying and thankful for every day I'm alive
With my family and friends I love.

The above poem was written by a male student finishing his coursework in Early Childhood Education at the University of Nebraska at Omaha. His background is different than the urban students he serves, but the themes are universal.

Chapter 8

Teacher Education Students Share Their Voices: The Exponential Effect of Transformation

by Evangelina "Gigi" Brignoni

I think that when you share with others, you are able to be more like yourself. If you are able to make a connection with just one person I think that the writing is much more beneficial. Overall, I think that sharing your writing helps the writer and others understand that we are more alike than different. It is so good to know that others feel the way that you do; when you do not share your writing, how would you ever know this?

Raimond Wojtalewicz
student from University of Nebraska at Omaha

It is the final day of class in the Teaching Reading and Language Arts course where twenty-two pre-service teaching candidates have just shared personally relevant and poignant children's books. The stories they created follow the format provided in *Authors in the classroom*: *A Transformative Education Process* (Ada & Campoy, 2004). It is the culmination of a semester of incorporating theory with practice and a celebration of each other. When I listen to my students' stories, I learn just a little more about who they are, the values they hold, and the risks they are willing to take by sharing a part of their lives with others. This chapter will focus on one semester and the lessons learned by one teacher education classroom community about our writing and how it transformed our lives.

Spring 2008 has been an incredible semester for the University of Nebraska at Omaha. Alma Flor Ada and F. Isabel Campoy spent one week in the Omaha community speaking to elementary and middle school students. For one hour, they spoke to my students about their transformative work. As Alma and Isabel shared their wisdom and experiences, my awe-struck students were mesmerized by their passionate voices. This private and personal conversation helped make the text come alive.

Role of Teacher Education in Transformative Pedagogy

Before I begin, I thought it might be wise to share my perspective on the role of teacher education to prepare future educators. I see the role of teacher education as helping teacher candidates work within the parameters of the educational system while still placing students at the center of the curriculum by teaching to the students' needs and fostering high-achieving students, positive learners, and critically-thinking individuals. I see the pre-service teacher as a beacon of hope. This hope is grounded in educational theories such as constructivism, transformative pedagogy, multiculturalism, and feminism. One responsibility of teacher education faculty is to present what is pedagogically sound and guide the teacher candidates to negotiate what is in the best interest of their pupils by working within the system and making informed choices that effect change and help students in the long run. Another role of teacher education faculty is to walk the walk by modeling how to teach and then deconstructing the lesson one rehearsal at a time. My role as a faculty member in a Teacher Education Department is to share how "Literacy is central to the on-going struggle for democracy and self-determination" (Yagelski, 2000, p.3). And finally, teacher education is about the rehearsal or practice before future teachers have their own classrooms. This chapter is about the rehearsal.

Some Background Information and Purpose of the Course

Our "Teaching Reading and Language Arts" methodology course is designed to prepare elementary and middle school pre-service educators to become successful practitioners of language arts. A practicum experience is an essential component of the course, and my students teach eight language arts lessons in an urban school where there are students of diverse backgrounds including Whites, Latinos, African Americans, Native Americans, Sudanese, Somalians, and Asians. The school's vice principal collaborates and assigns the university students a classroom based on their grade preference from kindergarten through sixth grade. There are many standards associated with this methodology course, but the ones that resonate most with me are the standards dedicated to writing, editing, and voice. Alma Flor Ada and F. Isabel Campoy (2004) share the perspective that "the process of encouraging authorship in the classroom and in the home, begins with the freedom of our own voices" (p. 15).

Let's Talk about the Writing Rehearsal

The very first writing assignment I ask my students to compose is a "By Myself" poem. It is an assignment found in *Authors in the Classroom: A Transformative Education Process* (Ada & Campoy, 2004). I begin by sharing the poems by Eloise Greenfield and F. Isabel Campoy and inform my students that they are going to compose one about themselves. I also divulge that they will be sharing with a partner in class (pair share), and eventually their course writings become part of a class anthology that they will receive during mid-term conferences.

Everything is disclosed at the beginning of the lesson; plus it is included in the course outline, so there are no surprises. I preface the course by mentioning that the more a teacher writes, the more classroom students will write. I also announce that I will be composing my own "By Myself" poem. I firmly believe that if I state that writing is important, I need to model it, too. I have four versions of a "By Myself" poem created in Nebraska. This is the most recent one:

By Myself
by Gigi Brignoni (Spring, 2008)

When I am by myself
I am a dancer
Moving to the tunes of Hector Lavoe
"Che, che Colé
Qué bueno es"
I am the joy
That dancing brings.
I am Anita of West Side Story
Strong, loving and Puerto Rican
I am warm and bright
And ready to take on the World.
But when I open my eyes
I am happy to be me
Alone with my memories
That help me remember
I am a dancer.

Before the students compose their "By Myself" poems, I ask them to close their eyes as I walk them through some visualization exercises using the five senses and answering the five W's. For example, I may say, "Close your eyes and breathe deeply. You are in a special place by yourself. What do you see? Are there any colors that are illuminating? Where are you now? Are you in a place that relaxes you or stirs you to do something? Who do you see? Do you hear any sounds? What do you feel?" After a few minutes of peaceful visualization, I ask the students to list what went through their minds as I spoke. Once they feel they have recovered their memory, they begin their poem.

Here are two examples reprinted with the students' permission:

By Myself
by Sarah Stevens
When I am by myself
And I close my eyes
I am strong like a storm
And also gentle like a light breeze
I am trustworthy like a good friend
And imaginative like a child
I am generous like my Mom
And courageous like my Dad
I learn from the past
When I look to the future
I am proud of what I've become
And when I open my eyes
What I want to be
Is me.

ME
by Krista Wickersham
With a hard outer coating, I am strong
But as tension grows
I break, I chip.
There are many different sides of me
And sizes, And colors.
Sometimes empty, and sometimes full of life.
In comparison, my life and who I am
Is most like a sea shell.

Why Have I Selected These Two Poems to Share in This Section?

There were so many poems to choose from that it was difficult to determine which ones to include. I shared the poems from an early childhood teacher candidate and a candidate whose goal is to teach in middle school. Both of these students went through the same visualization exercises and developed their own version of a "By Myself" poem. I gave them a format to follow, but it did not limit their creative potential. Sarah shared her perspective, "When we were writing poetry in class, I like how you gave us an optional format to follow. I think this would benefit students because it will give them an example to go off of, and also allow those students who want to be more creative the ability to do that" (an e-mail reply dated May 27, 2008).

"By Myself" poems allow students to open up, especially those students who regularly don't speak up or participate in classroom discussions. On a more personal level, my particular poem hides who I am in a more concrete object. This can also be helpful for those kids who don't want directly to come out and talk about themselves. They can disguise some object as having qualities that they have without being up front about it" (Krista Wickersham, June 2008).

During this rehearsal, I provide a model, and then the students choose poetry frames, free flow poetry, or templates. What both students share is that in poetry there is a foundation, but it doesn't limit your voice or the way you interpret the assignment. All students write and, as they write, they discover the best way to organize their thoughts and write poetically. From the beginning of the assignment, the students encounter the safe space to create. Within fifteen minutes, something has been put down on paper – the pre-write, the first draft, or the thoughts. Then, students partner up. After they share their "By Myself" poem with one other classmate, we debrief the experience. We discuss how to adapt, modify, and prepare the lesson for each grade level (K-6), and differentiate for special needs and/or English learners. The templates provide a scaffold and lower the anxiety for the reluctant writer. We focus our discussions on the current practicum assignments, understanding that everything they rehearse in the class can be done in their future classroom.

Sharing an Anthology in a Teacher Education Classroom

Every semester, I hold mid-term conferences with each student in this course. For fifteen minutes, I am personally able to connect and learn something about each student – what their plans are, how their practicum assignment is going, what challenges they may have, and how the course is going for them. At the end of the conference, I hand each of them the anthology. Every semester, as editor, I dedicate the anthology to the poets who contributed their work; this semester, I chose to dedicate the anthology to Alma and Isabel:

"We dedicate this anthology to Alma Flor Ada and F. Isabel Campoy whose work has inspired us to share our stories and our small moments with students at Indian Hill Elementary and in our future classrooms."

I showed each student the dedication, and they agreed that it was appropriate, especially since I noted that during their visit I would give them our anthology as a token of our appreciation. Receiving the anthology with the added knowledge that Alma and Isabel would have their own copy surprised my students. As in previous semesters, the pre-service teachers appeared pleased, surprised, grateful, and appreciative to receive the anthology. This semester, they were honored that Alma and Isabel accepted our gift with love, appreciation, and humility. This moment will forever be imprinted in this class's memory.

From the pedagogical and practical standpoint, I always want to know the impact this anthology building has on them and whether or not they will implement a similar strategy in their practicum assignment or future classroom. So, I asked them and here are a few of the comments:

Raimond Wojtalewicz wrote:

When I received the anthology during conferences I felt that someone really did care about our writings and what we as a class had to say. I felt that I had accomplished a task without even knowing that I had. When reading others I noticed that I had a lot in common with others or could at least show some empathy to what they were feeling. Many cultures in our world are so different yet many people go through the same challenges and face the same daily tasks. This really opened my eyes to that.

Kelly J. Labenz wrote:

> Participating in writing the poetry books was a highlight for
> everyone I believe. When we were informed and instructed on how
> to write the poems we were excited to get started, and then when
> we were told at the end of the lesson that they were going to be put
> in a poetry book, that escalated our excitement and we were even
> more excited to be participating! I used that method when I had my
> class write their poems for their poetry books, and they were eager
> to get started with making their books.

And finally, Karla A. McPhillips.

> When I received the anthology during midterm conferences, I was
> pleased to be able to have such a unique artifact. I was happy to
> carry different writings from my classmates.

These students share many of the same sentiments as their peers. Students are
negotiating the complexities of life through literacy moments (Yagelski, 2000), while
liberating their voices (Ada & Campoy, 2004). This is the rehearsal moment that I hope
students remember – their feelings about receiving a published anthology with their
poetry and what they can glean from each other's poems. If half of the students work
this moment into their curriculum, the exponential effect will be astounding. Listening
to students' life experiences is very liberating. Hayes, Baruth, and Kessler (1998) write,
"A teacher creates an environment for learning, Freire says, which builds upon the
knowledge and experience that a child brings to the classroom" (p.3). Sharing classroom
published works also sparks the students' interest in writing (Hayes, Baruth & Kessler,
1998, p.10). This adds another layer to the exponential effect of transformation.

Rehearsing Other Literacy Moments

Before I became a college professor in a teacher education program, I was a
staff developer in an urban school district in California. I noticed how some teachers
did not take the time to structure writing into their school day. I would attribute this
lapse to the notion that the teachers themselves did not write and, therefore, did not love
writing enough to motivate their own students to write. Therefore, as a teacher educator,
I make a conscious effort to have students write in various genres such as "Where I am
From" poems, "I Wish" lists, letters of introduction, and expository essays. Again, I

always share one of my own written pieces with the students to give the blocked writer an example of a particular genre. What results is usually a sample that is thankfully better written than mine.

Where I Am From
by Raimond Wojtalewicz

I am from 2, one German and one Pollack
I am from my mom and dad, dedicated to the government
Omaha, From D.C. – there is where it began for me
I am from the speg o cans, and the pool all day
I am from the parts of D.C. where you don't want to be
I am from family members in and out
I am from a school where I was the only one
I am from a team who accepted me
Black top courts with chained nets with a ball that did not have air, that is me
I am jealous to see others' houses who let me in
I am scared to touch things I cannot afford
I am moving from my home, I am a farmer now that is what I am told
I disagree and don't want to be
I am no longer the only one, where did they all go
I am where school lunches are amazing
No longer having speg o's.
Steak, chicken and breakfast for dinner, maybe it is not so bad
As time goes by and I get older more things become clear.
Life is better and dad is at home and we have 2 reliable cars
High school is here and times are still getting better
Football, basketball, golf and baseball is who I am. Dedicated to many things I love,
Which I am not used to.
I did not inhale is what I heard.
Now in college with a purpose in life
A life changer this is what I am
Youth with problems like guns and drugs
Helping them is who I am
My son, my wife, my job, my life that sums it up for me--this is my life.

The above poem is a brilliant example of a "By Myself" poem by a young man who will become an incredible instructor of middle school students.

How I Model the Where I Am From Poetry Exercise

I first share a poem that I wrote in the year 2000 with high school students in a California school district. I model how I have shared the poem with fourth graders, and we deconstruct it by looking for the people that appear, the foods that were important to me, words that were said, and my surroundings. Then, I give the pre-service teachers a four-square graphic organizer that they fill in with memories of their childhood. Once they generate enough recollections, they follow the format of "Where I Am From" or design their own. These poems are saved in their writing notebooks for further revision. Raimond selected his poem to be included in the anthology. One or two other students decided to create a children's book based on their "Where I Am From" poem. There is no limitation to what can be done with a first draft of any genre.

The Children's Book

The last assignment of the semester is the Children's Book. At the beginning of each semester, the course outline states the nature of this assignment and the date it is due – last session of class. The children's book is based on Ada and Campoy's text, *Authors in the Classroom: A Transformative Education Approach*, and a rubric is provided. It is only fair that students understand the parameters of the culminating writing activity. Below is the rubric that the students receive. Even though the rubric guides the format and the work, the content ideas may be found in one of the drafts, a tribute to family, or their own experience. Some students from previous semesters have given me their own books with the knowledge that they serve as examples for future students. I feel honored to have them in my possession.

Table 8.1
The Children's Book Rubric

	3	2	1
Content/Voice	The author's voice is very strong. The author shares something personal about his/her life.	There is an adequate voice. It is not clear if the author is sharing a personal vignette.	Fictional tale. Book does not reflect any aspect of personal experience.
Intended Audience	It is evident that the author has young children in mind and the book can be part of a classroom library.	The author's intended audience is very general.	The author's intended audience is older than elementary school.
Presentation	Vivid pictures, strong voice, captivating story line.	Adequate pictures and/or illustrations. Text matches pictures. Satisfactory story line.	It has the appearance that no time or thought was put into the book's production.
Format	The format of the book follows the format given in class. Very well organized.	The format of the book is well organized. One or two sections of the format are missing.	Disorganized. No format followed.
Conventions	Very accurate and precise spelling and punctuation.	Five or more conventions need repair.	It is obvious that the work was not re-read for editing or revision. Hence, no editing mistakes or inappropriate conventions were repaired.

An example of a children's book is by Nancy Voris, a future educator and school librarian. She titled her book *My Hero*. Nancy wrote about her "bestest" friend, her mother. It is a touching tribute to a strong woman who in her later years died of cancer. As Nancy puts it, "And because she loved us, we are happy. That is her legacy to us. She will always be our hero!" What is impressive about this book is that Nancy read this children's book to her kindergarten students. They wanted to know about Nancy's mother and the impact she had in her life. What transpired next is that the kindergarten students wanted to write about someone important to them and, in their kindergarten way, they did.

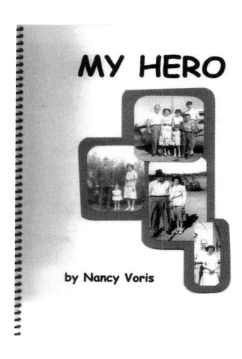

Photograph 8.1

What Made This Children's Book an Appropriate Book for Kindergarten?

       Nancy included family pictures in a sequential format. The students were able to see when Nancy was a baby and how she grew up. They had a personal connection with the author. Family books and books about mothers are usually big hits with younger children, and Nancy involved the kindergarten students in her writing process steps. She would share some information about the book she was creating, and the students were eager to see the end product. Finally, they knew that they would create their own book and, as future kindergarten authors, they celebrated Nancy's progress.

I liked to help my Mom.

I did the dishes ...

and helped her with the laundry.

Photograph 8.2   Photograph 8.3

As her language arts instructor, I am honored that Nancy Voris gave me her book and allowed me to share some of it in this chapter:

> I was not sure how my kindergartners would relate to the book when
> I read it to them at our next class. They listened intently to my story,
> laughing with me when we looked at the old photos, and sympathizing
> with me when I talked about my father's death and my mother's illness. I
> was overwhelmed at the end of my story when the entire class broke out
> in applause. (Nancy Voris, May 2008)

Nancy followed the format by providing a title page, creating a publishing house, a dedication page, the story and, as a conclusion, the "about the author" information. Just as in Nancy's model, most of the books that my students create look professional.

Concluding Remarks

I impress upon my students how student writing can tell us what students know. If this is so, why not provide authentic reasons to write in the classroom? These few strategies do more than inform teachers of their practice. It gives them spaces to share what they know – their own life experiences. It is also about taking risks of sharing personal information with others. When we share personal information with students, they start to take risks, too. This is the exponential component mentioned in the title. This is why I am in teacher education - when one teacher candidate is inspired to structure writing in a school day, thousands of students will become writers.

- "When I become a teacher, I will continue to read my story and encourage my students to tell theirs," states Nancy Voris.
- "A student's voice should be shared with others," reminds Krista Wickersham.
- "Many people may come across as not being the writing type but when they write on paper, it just flows and you can not tell who those people are without them telling their stories, I use the example of what Wade wrote and the kid who speaks with sign language. That book was so strong and yet surprising that you just had to say,'Aw, that is so cool. A great job of thinking outside the box,' " comments Raimond Wojtalewicz.
- Kelly Labenz adds, "I observed a great deal from the poems written by the students in my class. Not all of them wrote the same type of poem, and they all included small pieces of personal information. That was a good way to add character to the poems and individualized the author. That is one of the things I

tried to implement for my students. I encouraged my students to use their ideas or better word usage to give a more personal feel to their poetry."

And the rehearsal continues. Another semester will begin and a whole new classroom of pre-service teachers will have an opportunity to write their version of "By Myself," "Where I Am From" and a children's book. I look forward to meeting new class members, listening to different voices and, perhaps, planting the seeds of inspiration for structuring writing in the school day. My students' liberated voices have been heard and will be shared with their future students.

This is why I love what I do.

Table 8.2
Prompts or Procedures on Writing a Children's Book

Topic	Suggestions
Ideas	Look for ideas from published children's books. Ideas can be found in *Authors in the Classroom.* (Ada & Campoy, 2004)
Audience	Decide who is the intended audience (kindergarten, primary grades, middle school, secondary, your family, etc.).
Interests	What do you want to share with others? (A small moment in your life, your poetry, a life changing moment, an alphabet book on the community, etc.)
Begin writing	Follow the writing process. Write the first draft. Share with someone. Get feedback. Revise. Edit. Rewrite. Feel good about the piece.
Format the book	Include title page. Create your own publishing house. Use the copyright symbol © with the publishing year. I usually use "Between Many Worlds" as my publishing house.
Dedication page	To whom will you dedicate the book? This is a very life-affirming act and validates loved ones.
Organization	Decide how to organize the book. What text will be on what page? (Will there be pictures, photos, illustrations, icons, montage, etc?)
About the author page	What will you share that makes you unique? (Ideas to include – size of family, your birth order, interests, hometown, aspirations, interest in topic, etc.)
Binding	How will you bind the book? (Spiral binding, stapling, brads, etc.)
Presentation	Will you share this book with your class? Will you make copies to keep in the classroom library? Will this book serve as a model for your students' future books?

Questions for "Teacher Education Students Share Their Voices: The Exponential Effect of Transformation" by Gigi Brignoni

1. Why is listening to students' stories important?

2. Why should teachers be grounded in educational theories?

3. How does sharing one's voice encourage an author to be more powerful? What are ways in which you have facilitated this process?

4. There are some agencies dedicated to helping teachers become better facilitators of the writing process in the classroom. For example, the National Writing Project based in Berkeley, California offers professional development opportunities throughout the nation. www.nwp.org. How could professional development in writing support your continuing growth as a practitioner?

Chapter 9
Preparing Pre-Service Spanish Bilingual Teachers To Develop a Vision for Transformative Education

by Josephine Arce

I know that it is not the English language that hurts me, but what the oppressors do with it, how they shape it to become a territory that limits and defines, how they make it a weapon that can shame, humiliate, colonize.

bell hooks

Bilingual-Latina/o pre-service teachers are caught between their commitment to teach in bilingual programs and the reality that bilingual programs are continually under attack and being dismantled at all levels of education. The dilemma stems from the xenophobia of the dominant cultural and ideological hegemonic structures that have waged war against bilingual students, Latino immigrants, bilingual education and bilingual educators (Arce, Luna, Borjian, & Conrad, 2005).

Research Aim

This study engaged pre-service Spanish bilingual credential candidates through a course content that promoted dialogues about Latino's self and collective identities, socio-economic and political issues, power relations within educational settings, and in society at large. The course titled EED 737 Teaching Social Studies, Social Justice and Literacy, Grades 3-6, was a culminating course in a three-semester program. Students explored Latino's history of resistance in the United States: they uncovered the significance of historical memory as a form of power, and they participated in critical dialogical as a method to name the problems, critically reflect on them, and act upon these issues. They learned how to use effective literacy strategies that support learners to become critical thinkers. Specifically, the questions that guided the course content were: What did it mean to develop critical consciousness that supported a bilingual-bicultural transformative perspective? How were theory and practice both connected in the course, presentations, discussions and lectures?

Purpose of the Study

The purpose of the study was to gain an understanding of how one cohort consisting of fourteen Spanish bilingual pre-service students in the San Francisco State University, Department of Elementary Education grappled with the complex relationship between critical theory, critical literacy, equity, California state mandates, teaching practices, and sometimes, the disconnect between critical pedagogy and effective teaching learned in the course and in their field experiences. This course is an integral part of the SFSU Teacher Education Multiple Subject Credential Program; however, the content focus and transformative aspect were attempts to prepare Spanish bilingual candidates to expand their social and political consciousness and learn how to teach against the grain. The primary goal was to plant the seeds towards embracing a transformative educational perspective for these future teachers.

Specific Aims of the Study

1. To provide a focused process where Spanish bilingual pre-service candidates engaged in critical dialogue that supported a transformative philosophy of education.
2. To have the participants enter into a process that highlights distinct modes of consciousness: self-identity, analyses of power relations, understanding of resistance theories, and the construction of a framework for transformative education (Darder, 1995; Darder, Baltodano, & Torres, 2009; Giroux, 1983).
3. To support the development and cultivation of a collective consciousness as an essential component to the formation of a bilingual/bicultural identity (Darder, 1995, p.323).
4. To provide conditions for the development of a collective perspective within pre-service Spanish bilingual teacher candidates to strengthen their knowledge base regarding the history and politics of Latinos in the United States.
5. To have this research project serve as a framework for future bilingual teachers to replicate critical dialogues in their own classrooms as a method to guide Latino bilingual students to empower themselves.
6. To analyze the role of language within the context of power. The course was conducted bilingually with the intent to demonstrate that there are multiple linguistic forms that are as valuable as academic Spanish and English.
7. To analyze the messages conveyed through adopted textbooks and prescribed curriculum. I used an alternative book, *The Line Between Us* (Bigelow, 2006) that focused on US and Mexican immigration issues, integrated children's literature

focusing on Latinos, showed documentary films, played Spanish and bilingual protest music, and presented slides on Latino/Chicano art.

8. To move beyond the limitations found in teacher education programs where traditionally bilingual courses focused on non-political methods and diversity courses from a "victimization" perspective. This course explicitly focused on a history of struggle, resistance, and successes.

9. To provide a future professional network to break the potential of teacher isolation. Five candidates actively searched and obtained jobs at the same immersion school site. They continue to support each other.

Theoretical Framework

This research is guided by the work in critical, social, and political theories as they pertain to bilingual education and critical pedagogy. Hegemony, as defined by Gramsci, exists in systems viewed as democratic where the dominant class exercises its will through non-coercive modes, by exercising control of the mores, ethics, values, and standards of the society as a whole. Gramsci stated that the dominant class is able, with the alliance of many interest groups such as intellectuals, educators, unions, politicians and the media, to articulate the norms by which other socio-economic groups live (as cited in Hoare & Smith, 1971, pp. 56, 245-246).

Hegemony uses non-coercive modes by granting concessions to oppositional forces (Giroux, 1983). An example was the governmental support for the implementation of bilingual programs and the training of bilingual teachers. These concessions grew out of the Civil Rights Movement when Chicanos demanded the right to have bilingual education. While the government has conceded to this alternative educational program, it has also worked to undermine its success through multiple layers of bureaucratic institutions. Educational institutions have played a major role in undermining the progressive elements of bilingual education. Teacher education bilingual programs have shifted from the initial goals of the late 1970s and early 1980s that were designed to promote and maintain biculturalism, build strong bicultural group and individual-identity, and develop highly proficient bilingualism and biliteracy.

Many bilingual education courses have dwindled, providing only methods courses that focus on the teaching of reading in the primary language and mostly focusing on sheltered English instructional strategies. Along with this shift toward more methods and mainstream standardization, the courses are implementing California's high stake assessments that are mandated to Teacher Education Programs. Since 2009, pre-service teachers are assessed through Performance Assessment for California Teachers (PACT). This assessment appears as a reflective, high quality criterion, but the reality is that students find themselves focusing on the procedures to pass, with less focus in the course content, compounded by the reality that if they do not pass any segment of the PACT assessment, they must go through a process of remediation. Clearly, passing the high stake tests is a priority for all students. They are constantly stressed. The faculty is caught in the dilemma of how much pedagogy they can address, while simultaneously preparing them to pass all the components of PACT. Along with this "high stakes" test, prior to entering the Multiple Subject Credential Program, they must pass the California Subject Examinations for Teachers (CSET) and the California Basic Educational Skills Test (CBEST). When they complete the reading methods courses, they must take the Reading Instruction Competence Assessment (RICA). These are expensive tests that many potential bilingual candidates cannot pass in their first attempt. One needs to raise the question, "Who is profiting from all the tests?" This trend toward high stakes testing for credential candidates de-emphasizes content and urgent social issues in our courses, so how are we to prepare teachers to teach in urban schools? Specifically, bilingual teacher education programs need to revitalize bilingualism, biculturalism and provide settings to support proficient biliteracy.

As political trends influence educational regulations and policies, the state holds teacher education credential programs accountable to follow those mandates. These regulations result in emphasizing standards and methods classes while limiting opportunities for students to fully engage in intellectual discourse and exploration on issues about politics, policies, and educational theories in the United States. Bilingual programs within teacher education face even more limitations because they offer few courses that focus specifically on issues pertaining to bilingual communities. Bilingual candidates have limited access to participate in building a collective vision for a democratic, transformative bilingual and bicultural education. These political decisions impact all credential students.

Darder (1997) states that de-intellectualized environments in teacher credential programs convert pre-service teachers into technicians. This has even a greater impact on bilingual candidates because most come to the profession with the aim to help their communities, not only to teach children. These students run the risk of viewing themselves as little more than skilled workers if the credential courses are void of addressing the historical struggles and the pro-activism found in culturally and linguistically diverse communities. Bilingual programs implementing critical pedagogy can act to counter hegemonic directions. They offer teacher education courses that guide future teachers in bilingualism, history of resistance, critical theory, and developing alternative visions for transforming education (Darder, 1995; hooks, 1994, 2003; McLaren, 1981; Sleeter & McLaren, 1995). Bilingual educators who are grounded in critical pedagogy are able to create opportunities for their students, and themselves, to develop their voices and navigate in realms of possibilities for change (Reyes & Halcón, 2001).

While reductionist approaches to teacher education programs are impacting all future teachers, there are greater risks for bilingual teachers because of the anti-immigrant political climate and anti-bilingual policies from government agencies, with the collaboration of neoconservative media, which penetrate into the mindset of the average citizen. If bilingual teachers continue to reproduce the mainstream curriculum and conservative perspectives, bilingual and bicultural children and youths will continue to encounter barriers to flourishing as critical learners. Critical bilingual educators at all academic levels can be the advocates and mentors to historically disempowered Latino students (Darder, 1997, p.332).

Critical Pedagogy

I was searching for teaching approaches that would not control the learning situations. I applied a Freirean critical pedagogical approach by posing socio-political questions to inspire dialogue that would hopefully lead to self-reflections, group dialogues, then individual and group praxis (Freire, 2004; Shor, 1987). Freire's critique of traditional education is that when used as an instrument of control, it inhibits the development of critical consciousness. Specifically, the banking concept of education is designed to subject groups of people to believe that they are recipients or spectators while other forces (generally the dominant class' views) interpret the world for them, controlling knowledge and holding power over them (Darder, Baltodano, & Torres, 2009; Freire, 2004). Freire's theory for a critical pedagogy examines the relationship between individuals and the world; a person is not merely in the world as a spectator, but is deeply immersed as a participant by naming experiences in the world, living as active beings and recreating new social, economic, and political relationships (Freire, 2004).

Central to Freire's theory of liberation is the notion of dialogue, which is the encounter between people who engage actively in their environments and the world. Hence, dialogue occurs between those who want to break the silence by naming their experiences within the context of history and power relations (Freire, 2004). Dialogue, then, requires authenticity, critical reflection, and unified action. It is the essence of a liberating educational process. Through dialogue the possibilities exist for participants to develop social consciousness or refine their views in ways that allow for new construction of knowledge. Participants began to understand that conflicts, whether at the community or global levels, are not merely isolated events--they have a historical nature. Through dialogue we are able to identify the problem and name it together, in order to construct new knowledge. Dialogue is not merely talk or polemics to be consumed by the participants. It is fundamentally the search for voices to identify the source of problems, to reflect deeply upon those issues that keep us subjugated, and to engage in praxis that leads to transformation (Freire, 2004).

Perhaps one of the most significant aspects of dialogue is a necessary love for humanity. According to Freire's own passionate writings on the matter, dialogue cannot exist in the absence of a profound love for the world and for people (p. 89). It is this deep conviction and passion for a socially just world where I have grounded myself in a liberation theory that also demands praxis. The alliance between theory and praxis is an understanding that social change emerges from on-going interaction of reflection, dialogue and action (Darder, Baltodano, & Torres, 2009). These scholars point out that theory illuminates human activity and serves to provide us with a deeper understanding of the world as we experience and name it, opening into the realms of possibilities for a better world. They point out that when theory is cut off from practice, it becomes abstraction or "simple verbalism, while practice separated from theory becomes ungrounded activity or 'blind activism' " (Darder et al., p. 13). As the professor of this course, I believed this was the right time to support students' development in critical pedagogy based on Freire's dialogical method.

Class Sessions – Linking Theory with Practice

In the first session, I explained that my intentions were to have dialogues about our history as Latinos within the United States. It was not an autobiographical course, but one where we could address issues of the Latino communities and naturally integrate our experiences as they related to the broader social issues. Nieto (2003) proposes that environments or assignments that ask teachers, in this case pre-service candidates, to reflect upon their personal experiences should be used more profoundly as a step toward thinking how they can be more effective with their students.

In every session, I used literacy strategies with the candidates that could also be used in a classroom with children. This form of modeling and practice allowed them to experience how instructional strategies are linked with the theory of critical pedagogy.

I began each session with a read aloud strategy using children's literature or listening to Spanish or bilingual protest songs. Students were excited to see many children's books representing Latinos. Logically speaking, they wanted to be informed about books they could use in their classrooms. I exposed them to a wealth of children's literature with a focus on Latinos. Initially, I encouraged them to explore, read to each other, and to share what they liked about the books. I then introduced them to the guidelines presented by the Council on Interracial Books that advise teachers on how to select texts that are anti-biased. I posed open-ended questions after their initial exploration. Here are a few samples:

1. How were Indians portrayed during the pre-Columbian period in social studies textbooks and in a popular children's book such as *Encounter* by Jane Yolen (1992)?
2. How are Latina girls and Latina women generally portrayed in children's books?
3. How are Latinos' cultural markers or interactions represented in children's literature?
4. How are social struggles interpreted and whose point of view is presented?

Through their opportunities to review the anti-biased guidelines, respond to open-ended questions, re-read children's literature, and deconstruct the illustrations and the subtle messages, my students were astonished and in some instances outraged by their discoveries. They had to shift from the joy of seeing so many children's' books representing Latinos to becoming readers with more critical interpretive lenses. They realized that they had to question the view of authors who were perhaps not from the Latino culture and reflected a mainstream political perspective.

By re-reading *Encounters* a group of students decided that they would dramatize the encounter between the Taino Indians and Columbus and his troops offering a counter interpretation to Yolen's text. This group demonstrated that adult Tainos did not passively relinquish their society to the Spanish conquistadors. The students enthusiastically combined their research and the performance to offer a counter narrative. By identifying the problem, they collectively applied a critical pedagogical approach that was radically different from a social studies teacher's guidebook that gives suggestions on how to teach about the Spanish Conquest.

In addition, I provided expository texts that focused on current topics affecting Latino communities. They read a news clip about Mexican immigration to the United States. I posed the question, "Why is Mexico poor?" instead of the common question asked within mainstream instruction, which is, "Why do Mexicans want to come to the United States?" and another question, "Who does NAFTA protect? (Bigelow, 2006) By shifting from the U.S. to the Mexican perspective, participants were able to consider alternative views that went beyond the dominant cultural stance. The students responded through quick-writes and shared response strategies. They also read the informative book for classroom teachers, *The Line Between Us* (Bigelow, 2006), which provides a current perspective on Mexico border relations with the United States. By modeling and letting them practice how to use literacy strategies such as graphic organizers to support writing responses, and then the value of orally sharing their responses, they were able to experience how children could benefit from these strategies. Equally important, they learned how to share their views within a community of learners. Listening to their peers allowed them to rethink and revise their own ideas. Sharing also contributed to raising their political consciousness. Through these practices, they associated critical dialogue with building a community. They recognized that a cohesive community could represent more than being respectful, kind and caring, but that it also has the potential to prepare participants as actors for social and political changes.

As the instructor, I believed that selecting higher level questioning forms could lead to more critical responses from the students. The participants responded in a highly positive manner, not only addressing my questions, but also, and more importantly, raising their own questions. They expressed their anger toward the public schools. They identified situations in which schools collaborate to keep mostly lower income people in schools with decreasing funds and selecting curriculum that lacks opportunities for critical discourse. They also recognized the significance for a teacher to be an intellectual and a cultural worker in order to provide alternative views to their students.

My willingness to let go as the main transmitter of knowledge and to follow more student-centered questions was exactly what I wanted them to do in their own classrooms. Collectively, the students and I wanted to experience organic learning rooted in critical dialogue and reflection (Freire, 2004). At the end of every six-hour session, we were excited, challenged and hopeful.

The selections of assignments and students' acceptance of the tasks were powerful indicators of successful teaching and learning. Students had to perform a dramatization of a Latino historical event. At first, they felt it was an impossible task, but I reassured them that my goal was to demonstrate that the focus was on investigation and process, not a major theater production. I made a conscious decision to invite my colleague, a Latino theater professor, to guide us through some basic steps on acting.

His contribution was significant because he spoke about Latino theater, our community in San Francisco, and Latin America's tradition of people's theater. His cultural funds of knowledge inspired all of us. As a result, the students eagerly engaged in producing outstanding skits. Each group selected its own topic. These topics reflected different historical events such as Taino Indians combating the Spanish Conquest, the resistance of Mexican women who were factory workers at the US-Mexican borders, the resistance movement of the Mexican people toward Whites who appropriated California, and a representation of the United Farm Workers Boycott that included Filipino farm workers.

All the students expressed how much they gained from this assignment as evidenced in their written evaluations, comments during the dialogue session, and in the final class meeting. The drama skits, for me, proved that a professor could incorporate alternative learning forms beyond reading and writing that may have more impact on students. Specifically, I witnessed that even the quieter students transformed into empowered individuals. Their actor's stance revealed an authentic connection to the historical event. The responses to assignments in and out of class were positive. In retrospect, the drama was a very demanding assignment, but perhaps the most rewarding. I was profoundly moved because the dramatizations provided a venue for students to investigate, draw their conclusions about historical events, and act out the resistance of a specific cultural group. The dramatization of historical events challenged Eurocentric interpretations of history and demonstrated that Latinos have responded to repression through organized opposition.

Language as Power

Another area that contributed to the success of the course stemmed from my teaching decision to validate the students' efforts to speak Spanish during class. The course shifted from Spanish to English and code switching (mixing both languages without losing the meaning or structure). One Anglo student stated in the dialogue how much she felt validated by me, that I accepted her Spanish. Others stated that this was the first course where they could speak Spanish freely. I intentionally made the decision to validate the different levels of Spanish fluency. My decision arose from the fact that some Latinos born and raised in the United States may have limited academic training in Spanish. They may experience shame when they do not have full command of high-level academic Spanish language and literacy. Their shame was amplified when they compared themselves to non-Latino Spanish speakers who were more familiar with grammatical rules and academic vocabulary. I wanted students to develop confidence to speak Spanish, witness models of academic Spanish, and interact in a low anxiety environment. Darder

(1997) states human beings are able to appropriate a multitude of linguistic forms and use them in critical and emancipatory ways. I supported the use of multiple forms of Spanish, while we also used standard forms. Students appreciated that I was non-judgmental and accepted their levels of Spanish fluency.

The Effectiveness of Critical Pedagogy: Evidence-Based Results

The prevalent themes that emerged from class discussions are reflected in their assignments and in the concluding dialogue:

Theme 1: Bilingual candidates viewed themselves as empowered through the collective community and felt more equipped to teach.

Theme 2: Bilingual candidates had a Spanish bilingual community of peers to share similar linguistic experiences. They used multiple forms of Spanish, code switching into both languages and used English when they read texts.

Theme 3: Bilingual candidates used their funds of knowledge and applied new information about Latino history and current affairs relying on critical pedagogy as their framework for discussions and written assignments. Students learned to critique texts and question inaccuracies of historical and current events.

Theme 4: As newly hired bilingual teachers, they participated in a dialogue with me. They responded to questions on whether they could apply critical pedagogy in their classrooms. They were also asked if they had to follow a prescriptive curriculum, and to describe how they were able to integrate ideas shared from the EED 737 bilingual course.

Student Reflections

Bilingual candidates viewed themselves as empowered through their peer community, and they felt more equipped to begin teaching. Students reported that three major assignments contributed to their knowledge and their confidence as teachers. First, after the third and seventh sessions, all the students wrote on their reflections, and that they gained new and more specific knowledge about Latinos in the United States because we used films, music, and expository texts related to Latino issues. Small groups held focused discussions and responded in writing to open-ended questions about films, music, and texts. They stated that they benefited from their discussions. As a whole class, we did not share all their responses, but each group selected the most significant questions and summarized their responses. This format allowed for sharing prior knowledge, interpreting newly acquired information, evaluating information, and expressing personal reactions. These discussions, combined with literacy strategies, contributed to refining or developing critical consciousness.

Secondly, students were highly positive about having the opportunities in class to practice literacy strategies that they could use in their classrooms. There was a significant difference, in this case, from simply practicing a strategy--they learned the strategies within the context of critiquing, deconstructing and reviewing texts that addressed Latino issues (historical and current).

Candidates also reviewed many samplings of children's literature noting the strengths, images, weaknesses, and underlying political messages of these books. Learning how to select and review children's books proved to be a valuable experience because they had political and cultural lenses to evaluate these books. Alanza noted that she used quality children's literature every day in her classroom, but many times she had to sneak it in during the language arts time because it was not part of the prescriptive reading/language arts lesson.

Thirdly, the assignment they were most apprehensive about, but one where they claimed to have made the strongest gains, was designing, planning, and presenting a thirty-minute dramatic skit. One group re-enacted the life of Indians in a California mission. Unlike most historical and fictional accounts where the Indians are domesticated or enslaved, this group told the story as Chicanos/Latinos visiting a mission as tourists; then they were magically transferred into the past to witness how Indians were colonized and forced into labor. The *tourists* witnessed how the Indians secretly organized and resisted. The message of this skit was that oppressed people never relinquish easily.

Educational Significance

The theoretical framework for the construction of a bilingual program that is grounded in critical pedagogy does have the potential to politicize, contest, develop and refine social consciousness, revitalize language and affirm cultural identity (Darder, Torres & Gutiérrez, 1997; McLaren, 2003). However, this one course proved to be successful and gave pre-service teachers an opportunity to examine, reflect, and initiate the process that they will use with their students, which will lead to the changes that are needed for their future. Giroux (1983) points out that the ultimate value of the notion of resistance is the degree to which it contains the possibility of galvanizing collective political struggle to confront the issues of power and social determination. Let us begin to imagine the possibilities to transform entire bilingual programs based on the constructs of critical theories and theories of resistance.

Limitations

The major limitation described by the students was that the course was only seven weeks long. Several students expressed not having enough time to process all the information. Karen was the only one who voiced that there were so many painful issues around race, class and power relations that could not be discussed in-depth.

My own interpretation of the limitations is to raise the question, "If the course consisted of a full fifteen weeks or was divided into modules, could there have been stronger evidence of the application of critical pedagogy or transformative practices in their classrooms?" Time was a major factor as I explored how much these new teachers internalize and apply their daily practices.

Conclusions

It is critical that bilingual teacher education programs take a leadership role in designing an entire program that guides bilingual teachers to develop a vision for transforming educational conditions with their students, the parents, and their communities. It is not enough to offer one course that promotes transformative education. I concur with Nieto (2009) that issues about linguistic and cultural diversity must be central in all teacher education programs.

In addition, teacher education programs need to push efforts to establish a systematic approach for continuing contact with graduating bilingual cohorts. Continuing contact would support a local network for bilingual teachers, and allow them to develop a collective consciousness as bilingual, critical educators. There are many possibilities that are beneficial from continuing contact that can lead to further understanding and practicing social justice within educational settings.

While the present political climate is extremely anti-immigrant and anti-bilingual, it is imperative to provide counter-resistance approaches based on theory and practice that prepare bilingual/bicultural teacher candidates and supply them with the critical knowledge and instructional strategies that cement a firm foundation, before they become the teachers in classrooms.

Chapter 10

Teaching for Voice:
Instructional Strategies for Empowering Youth

by Chris Knaus

*Teachers must learn how to recognize, honor, and incorporate the
personal abilities of students into their teaching strategies.*

Geneva Gay (2000)

This chapter demonstrates how critical race theory can be applied to a high
school writing class, and offers insight into how educators can develop curriculum and
teaching around student voice. I use critical race theory to frame course development
and pedagogy, and add my own self-reflection to illuminate how schooling must center
students in race-conscious ways that develop their critical voices. Developing voice,
in conjunction with developing critical writing and thinking skills, deepens student
engagement by showing students how school can be relevant to their lives. Such
engaging, voice-centered approaches require intensely reflective teaching in order
to transform classroom structures that are typically seen by urban youth as boring,
irrelevant, and fundamentally racist.

Centering student voice is essential precisely because students are often punished
for their reactions to negating, socially aloof curricula. Many urban students live a
world of turmoil; yet their schooling often denies their personal context. Because much
of standardized curriculum presents decontextualized information, urban students are
often taught to ignore their personal circumstances (Apple, 1993; Gay, 2000; Ladson-
Billings, 1994). Standardized curriculum, limited by public education's assessment-rich
but content-poor movement, is often developed and implemented in isolation from urban
contexts and is designed without the cultural knowledge of communities of color (Au,
2008; Knaus, 2007; Macedo & Bartolomé, 1999). Such prepackaged curricula present
knowledge that denies what urban students live through everyday; many urban students
in turn tend to disregard school. Yet, in order for schools to become viable and honor a
commitment to preparing students for democratic participation, schools must teach real-
world skills to help students navigate the world they live.

In this chapter, I frame critical race theory as a guide for responsive, voice-centered teaching. I provide a glimpse into students at an urban high school, and clarify the context these students live. I then demonstrate my teaching philosophy through capturing several lessons and interactions with students that are designed to help students reflect on their daily surroundings, while recognizing their experience as strength. I conclude by framing reflective, responsive practice as an integrated aspect of teaching that lets students and educators engage in serious dialogue as a way of modeling listening as teaching. This entire work rests upon the assumption that urban students live in communities of struggle, and that in order for schooling to reflect students, educators must share in the realities that students navigate daily.

The School

This chapter focuses on a particularly small urban high school in Northern California's Bay Area. The school is situated in a diverse, racially mixed neighborhood; a block from the school, freshly painted white picket fenced-in houses sit next to abandoned, boarded-up homes that offer temporary safety to drug-addicted homeless adults. A rundown liquor store faces the school, serving older African American and Latino men, who occasionally are seen staggering out, their fingers wound tightly around small brown paper bag-enclosed beverages. At the end of the block, two boarded-up, fenced-off, rundown buildings provide excellent cover for students to sneak off campus for a quick joint. The school is within walking distance of the subway station, but students take the much cheaper bus. The school is several blocks from the police station, yet a police car is regularly parked in front of the liquor store, facing the school. Directly across from the school is a boarded-up, litter-strewn public services health center, which serves low-income elders and drug-addicted clients. A newly constructed grass field rounds out the school's intersection, though the healthy-looking dark green grass is enclosed with an extra-tall chain-link fence reminding everyone to keep out.

While the school building is just a few years old, the school is not well-resourced, particularly compared to surrounding schools, which are touted as model schools. There is no computer lab, the science lab has no useful supplies, and most classrooms have no overhead machine, no Internet access, and no way for students to type up their papers at school unless they skip another class. There are relatively few books in each classroom, and most of the textbook sets are incomplete, tore up, or sit unused. Teachers generally bring their own dry erase pens and lock any other classroom supplies in their desks.

The school day begins at 8:30 in the morning; teachers generally arrive by 8:20 and students trickle in throughout the day. Outside of a sparsely attended afterschool program and the school's custodian, the school is empty fifteen minutes after the final bell rings at 3 pm. The gates around the school remain locked throughout the day, and visitors have to wait outside the gate until a student or staff person lets them in. The previous two years were without a full-time counselor, and no onsite educators were responsible for individualized educational plans (IEP's), despite the school's large special education population. The staff is young; most graduated college within two years, some were completing their teaching credential, and only two educators had specific training to address urban high school students.[1] Many of the well-intentioned teachers stood in the front of the classroom lecturing or handing out worksheets despite students sleeping, text messaging, or walking in and out of class. As I observed the teaching staff, I soon realized that most of the full-time teachers presented their curriculum aware of general student apathy, yet unaware of how to meaningfully engage students.

The Students

Most of the students attending the high school live within walking distance, though several students attend the school from up to twenty miles away. Seventy-five percent are eligible for the free and reduced lunch program, and 95% of the student body is African American and Latino. Most of the students are behind in credits and their English and math assessments are significantly lower than their Asian and White counterparts in the district. Many students are in danger of not graduating because they had not passed enough classes and because many had not passed the California High School Exit Exam. In order to graduate on time and prepare for the exit exam, these students often enrolled in two math classes, two English classes, a science class, and social studies each semester. Yet these students repeatedly demonstrate that they do not tolerate this narrowed curriculum (Jennings & Rentner, 2006; Knaus, 2007; Lynch, 2006; Oakes, 2005). On a typical day, the school was only half full, and some particularly disengaging courses often had only two or three students.

Below are brief glimpses into four students; they clarify realities that impact their capacity to engage in school. I tell these stories because most educators do not know students in this way; most of these students do not share these experiences with educators. Yet knowing who these students are is an essential foundation for any

---

1   One of those teachers' preparation was the culmination of several undergraduate courses I had taught that framed racism in schooling; yet these courses were prior to her decision to become a teacher and did not address content-level teaching.

potentially successful educational efforts. These stories are the result of students working hard to develop their voice and reflect student trust in me. They share some of who they are precisely because they feel such expression is necessary. In short, they need to talk through the issues that shape their lives, and through this class, they were able to create space to do that.

An Uncomfortable Alarm Clock

Rasheedah, an 18-year-old African American high school junior, clarified her before school routine several times in her journals. She wakes up at 4 am to tend to her mother, who will have just returned from her night shift cleaning job. She relates that some nights, her mother returns enveloped in a musty, lingering cloud; the familiar smell of unfamiliar men who rented her mother's body for still-not-enough money to pay rent. Rasheedah then wakes the still too-tiny baby, feeds her formula, and makes her mother dinner: scrambled eggs, freezer-burned sausage, and canned orange juice from the food bank. Her mother replaces Rasheedah's still warm outline in the bed they sleep in at opposite hours, and slips into an immediate deep sleep. Rasheedah then rouses her younger brother and sister, hurrying them into the shower, readying them for their school day. She fixes their breakfast – bowls of cereal topped with heaping spoonfuls of sugar. Just after six o'clock, she's rushing them out the door, always just barely catching the rusty public bus. The bumpy forty-five minute ride takes them deep through a blighted urban neighborhood, where she sleepily reflects on how the litter looks like what she imagines huge snow flakes skittering across barren still dark streets, but she has never seen snow. She corrals her siblings and heads them into their school, which opens never a minute before 7 am. Once they are safely at school, she crosses the street and waits for the return bus. She now has a forty-five minute ride back to where she can transfer to another forty-five minute ride to her school. Rasheedah usually makes it to school on time, but often falls asleep in her first period class.

Free or Reduced Lunch Program

Lucinda is a junior attending her fourth high school, and identifies as "Latina, Filipina, and sometimes Superstar." She comes into her first class after lunch looking exhausted, smelling pungent. Her eyes covered by sunglasses despite the relative darkness of the classroom, she plops heavily into her desk, tired and spent. I ask her if she is alright, and she nods her head sideways on her desk, but for the rest of the period, she raises her head only a few times. Each time, she looks around the room bewildered, as if lost in a dream, only to lay her head back down on the desk, arms at her side. After class,

I ask her to write what she had just gone through to make her so tired. She responds, "You don't want to know that," but the next day, gives me a note:

> Chris,
> I'm stuck. I don't like him, but I do. I can't be without him. He used to be so sweet, and we would smoke together during lunch. Then, sometimes, I would watch him play X-Box. Then, sometimes, we had S_X. But now, he smokes and then we have S_X and then he's done. We don't talk anymore. Its like I don't exist. I want things back to how they were. That's why I'm late back to school. I don't know what to do. I love him, but I don't, too. Yesterday, he didn't even let me smoke. So I snuck some when he went pee. I don't know what to do.

Hungry With No Dinner

Darnell is an 18-year-old African American high school senior with a slight build. He is attending his third high school, and writes about watching "imaginary sunsets from within my mom's white-walled mental health facility room." The bed takes up most of the space in her windowless room, so he sits at her side, as she drifts in and out of sleep. He isn't sure what's wrong with her, but for the past five years, she's been living in a home run by the county health department, and he's been at her side as often as he can be. His older sisters no longer visit, and his younger brother has been in juvenile hall for the past six months. He has worked upwards of thirty hours a week for the past two years to pay for his (and his brother, before he was incarcerated) tiny apartment. He rents out a room to a friend of his uncle, who pays rent with money he makes selling marijuana. Darnell is tired, but tries to stay awake until the nurse comes to feed his mother.

After she is fed, he hops on the bus and returns home. He writes: "The memorized bus stops slowly tick by as my belly rumbles out my waiting hunger." It is roughly 7 pm by the time he unlocks his front door, and he walks into a thick cloud of smoke. Darnell went into drug rehabilitation several years ago, and while he is comfortable around drug use, he has not used in over a year. He is soon talking with three of his roommate's friends, who already ate the package of hot dogs that would have been his dinner. "I order pepperoni pizza, try to settle down and write the short paper due in tomorrow's English class." His hunt-and-peck pointer finger takes forever to fill the screen, and after what seems like an hour, he comes out of his bedroom, hoping the pizza will be here soon so he can return to his paper. His roommate had come home and went, "taking my friends and my pizza with them." All that remains is the now-empty pizza box. He erupts in anger, punching the wall and cursing up a storm: "Anger pours out: Fuck! Fuck! Fuck! and I think of nothing but the pizza I aint got." Darnell grabs his cell phone, and tries to order another pizza. After being on hold for six minutes, he bitterly hangs up, knowing the pizza would take another hour anyway. He puts on his coat and heads outside to Kentucky Fried Chicken, a five-block walk in the rain. When he finally returns, he plops on the couch, spending the rest of the night watching re-runs, remembering the English paper only when his teacher asks for it during class the next day.

A Sleepless Night

Jasmyne, a high school senior, usually gets home as late as possible, to avoid having to face her Black step-mother, who continually dismisses her because, in Jasmyne's words: "I aint black enough, I got too much Native, too much Mexicana, not enough of the black that she is." She feels forced into the arms of her boyfriend, whom she spends almost every afternoon and evening with despite her worry that he takes their relationship too seriously. They began dating when Jasmyne was fourteen, and she used to hope that they will marry and have children. Recently, though, she has begun thinking that she no longer loves him; that she is in the relationship because she does not want to be alone, because she does not want to be home. What Jasmyne fears most is going to sleep at her step-mother's house, which she wishes she did not have to consider home.

On this particular night, she was home for dinner only because she had been fighting with her boyfriend, who had not called the previous three nights. "He don't call sometimes, and I hate that I care, but all I think about is phone ring phone ring phone ring and when it doesn't, I'm stuck where I don't want to be." Her step-mother had not returned home from work, and she was rummaging through the refrigerator, searching for something quick to cook so she could retreat to the sometimes comfort of the room she occasionally shares with her younger cousin. Jasmyne ate morsels of "tasteless food before grabbing a book" and lying on her bed, hoping for a rare quiet night. She was engrossed in the book when her quiet was shattered by her step-mother's screams: she was yelling at her father, who was home only every few weeks. "My hands shook as the words on the page shook" with nervous energy and the fear of what might happen on nights when they fought. Her father might drink himself to sleep, yelling at nothing and everyone before the alcohol passed him out. Once he was safely out, her step-mother, "a ball of drunken rage," would quietly stumble into Jasmyne's room. If her cousin was staying at the house, her step-mother might curse and quietly slip out of the room. But –

and this is the image she replayed every night for the past three years – her step-mother might instead lift back the covers and lay down next to her 17-year-old body. Jasmyne's step-mother had not done this in over a year, but some nights the fearful thoughts would not leave, keeping her awake throughout the night, "hoping for the phone call that wouldn't come."

"This Class is Real": Applied Critical Race Theory

I came into this school hoping to address, at least for one class of students, the list of reasons why such urban students should not consider schooling seriously. These students live complex, violent, oppressive realities, and their schooling often exacerbates their realities. Yet these are exactly the realities that educators must directly respond to, because if our classes do not help students navigate their worlds, then they will, as they demonstrate in urban schools across this country, simply leave school.[2] Against this context of urban schooling and student disengagement, I taught a writing class that centered on voice to capture the racist structures and realities framing these students' lives. Because I had been on campus regularly over the past year, I knew many of the students prior to them enrolling in my course; none wrote regularly, and none considered themselves "good" writers. Several were singers, rappers, graffiti artists, and dancers, so I knew they needed something to focus their expressive energies, and wanted to also help them think about their voices in an academic light. In talking with these students, I realized that their outside-of-school realities were much more pressing than anything educators could come up with; thus, I wanted to help them use their personal lives to develop critical voices.

I thus applied critical race theory to the classroom to frame my efforts to develop voice and narratives that challenge racism and the structures of oppression (Stovall, 2006). Critical race theory framed for me the notion that their everyday reality is rooted in racism (Delgado & Stefancic, 2001), and in order to address this reality, students must express what they live and see in tangible ways that encourage self-reflection. At the heart of critical race theory is an appreciation for storytelling, for those who are oppressed to express their insight into how society is structured, and how such structures impact their daily lives (Delgado, 1989). What makes critical race theory applied is the focus on expression of voice and narrative by students who are intentionally silenced

---

2   Depending on how one counts graduation statistics, California statewide graduation rates for African American and Latino students hover around 55-60%, though several urban bay area school districts have African American and Latino graduation rates well under 50% (Swanson, 2004).

by the everyday practices of schooling in the U.S (Swartz, 1992). Applied CRT thus challenges the status quo of mainstream U.S. colonial-based schooling by creating the structures through which student voice, particularly the voice of students of color, can develop, thrive, and express in culturally affirming and relevant ways (Stovall, 2006). Applied CRT argues that what educators need to know about why schooling fails can be found in listening to students (Cushman, 2003; Knaus, 2006; Shor, 1996; Stovall, 2006). Schooling, then, is applied critical race theory's foundation because schools are where communities of color have historically been told they are less intelligent and provided documentation of less economic worth than those who successfully navigate racialized academic barriers (Giroux, 2001; Ladson-Billings, 1999). Thus, "merit" is framed by critical race theory as a measure of whiteness or successful navigation of white values rather than a colorblind and culture-blind measuring stick of academic or intellectual prowess (Lipsitz, 1998).

By creating the structures through which voice can emerge, students can begin to develop their own understandings of knowledge to contradict the negative impacts of learning through a white-dominant form of knowledge that denies experiences that do not fit (Freire, 1970; Macedo & Bartolomé, 1999). Applied CRT thus frames knowledge as an intricate, multi-faceted set of stories that create our contested understanding of what happened and whom it happened to, rather than a simplistic notion of "his story" (Delgado, 1995; Yosso, 2005). Student voice, centers on personal experiences, told from the perspective that only one who lives the actual experiences can tell, thus becomes a central purpose of applied critical race theory-based education. In such schooling, student knowledge is framed as key to understanding oppression and to understanding how to foster democratic participation amongst systematically excluded populations.

The Class

I developed this class as a way to help students make sense of their lives through intense writing, and used critical race theory and cultural responsiveness to frame my approaches. Thus, this voice-focused writing course focused extensively on race and racism as lived experiences through Geneva Gay's four critical aspects of culturally responsive teaching: Caring, Communication, Curriculum, and Instruction (Gay, 2000). Through ensuring my pedagogy was deeply caring, I urged students to create their own space in our classroom, and in their writings. I continually affirmed student effort and writing, and just as continually urged students to express themselves more deeply, more in the language they use daily, with friends, at home (Gay, 2000; Lynch, 2006). I centered the ways in which students talk and communicate on a daily basis as a way to deepen their writings and to honor the ways they frame ideas. I created a curriculum that centered youth expression, and featured poets, musicians, comedians, and educators who regularly express their own critical voices (Fisher, 2007). And lastly, my pedagogy intentionally shared classroom power, where students shaped daily agendas, writing assignments, and ways of engaging in classroom dialogue (Stovall, 2006). My role, made clear throughout the course, was to ensure students were continually writing, continually editing, always pushing deeper to clearly communicate what they see and feel, and to ensure they respected each other and themselves in our shared space.

Class began with first day of the school year, and I introduced myself to the students. I shared that I stopped teaching college to work with them on their writing and voice. I shared poetry about my own troubled experiences as a student (Knaus, 2006). I provided the class with a two-page syllabus, and outlined expectations of daily presence and engagement, grading procedures, and the purpose of the class. I argued that "the class would be as deep as you all take us," and that I was there to help them develop and express who they are in ways that are "beautiful, powerful, and rooted in the world" they see. The purpose, I argued, was to help students develop their voices, and to say exactly what they want to, in their words. The first week was spent with students writing self-introductions and reading their introductions aloud to the class.

I also spent a lot of time setting and holding clear expectations about student behavior: if they wanted to sit in a circle, it was up to them to move the chairs each day (which they soon began to do each class). Each day began with a five to ten minute freewrite, and I encouraged students to choose the topic. We often then spent the class discussing what the students had written in response to the topic or prompt. Some days we focused on close writing assignments, where students practiced capturing feelings, items, experiences in thick, descriptive details (Jordan, 1995; Tannenbaum & Bush, 2005). Other days the class would center on a highly charged topic that was at the forefront of many students' minds. During these discussions, I joined in to ask critical questions and continue the dialogue, but for the most part, only jumped in when the dialogue went off track. Sometimes students became deeply emotional, and only when I noticed someone bordering on rage would I step in to provide space to let the rage out safely (often by having students freewrite on how they were feeling at that particular moment). I rarely jumped in, but when I did, I did so forcefully so that students understood that I would not allow anyone to be disrespected.

After weeks of intense discussion, powerful readings, poetry, films, and music that directly captured first-hand experiences with abuse, dismissal, and structural oppression, students began to put their deepest fears onto the page (and into the air of our classroom). I constantly asked students to push deeper, to clarify exactly what they wished to share. I demanded that students share raw words that they believe captured the depth, intricacies, and complexities they wanted to write about (Fisher, 2007; Tannenbaum & Bush, 2005). I reminded students that I was there to help their stories come out, to help edit the words they used, to never judge their experiences, but to help them work through the issues they wanted to express. And I shared my own voice every day, sharing insight into the violence I lived, into the rage I have built up around oppression.

At the beginning of each week, the class checked in about what we had been talking about, how our discussions went, and how their personal writing was going. Within a month, students began to share very personal details about their lives regularly, and read reflections and freewrites aloud, without any prompting. Students would then ask clarifying questions or provide feedback (such as "I feel you because my mom is like that, too," or "Why did you respond to her like that?"). I continually brought in guests that centered race-focused expression, all of whom also shared why they express their voices in the creative ways they do. This part was key; seeing, hearing, and feeling artists and educators express critical poetry or music and discuss why they dedicate their lives to expression helped model making a living off of creativity, but also normalized critical expression.

I also was very clear throughout the year that what was read aloud or discussed in our class remained confidential to our class. Students were not to talk about people in the class, but should discuss the topics we shared outside of class. The only way to fail the class, short of not doing the work, was to share information from the class outside our room or to dismiss someone in the class. And I made one clear example of a student in the beginning of the year to demonstrate that I was serious: one student was forced to take another class because he broke the shared agreement of confidentiality and mutual respect.[3]

---

3   The student had called several young women "bitches" in the class after they had shared their sexism-enlightening writing, and then later, after being confronted by the entire class, shared inappropriate details about another student who was being violently harassed by peers in the school. He was subsequently enrolled in another English course, and two months later, asked me to let him rejoin our class. The class decided against it, and invited him in so they could explain their decision (he declined the invitation).

Students wanted their voices to be heard as much as they wanted to write, and soon competed with each other to be the first to read aloud each day. This is not to say they did not resist writing, or that every student wrote when I asked them to. Indeed, there were many frustrating days when students slipped back into their traditional student roles, and I'd struggle to urge students to write, to listen to each other, to be present or at least write about why they could not be present. For every powerful explosion of voice into the classroom, there were two examples of what students began to call "words on a page": writing without much meaning. Students were engaged from the beginning, but this was not easy work.

In addition to writing and reliving some of their trauma, students were also getting intense feedback from me, which was initially overwhelming. Once a week, I provided feedback to written journals or papers students turned in, and they often had up to three pages of typewritten feedback to negotiate. Since students had so rarely received quality feedback (much less feedback that pushed them to clarify who they are) throughout their educational experiences, this both added to the difficulty, and became a source of dramatic encouragement. Students came to look forward to my feedback, and began to echo (and mock) my terminology: "Push on that" "Dig deeper" and "That is so vague" became commonplace as students began to accept that I was in the classroom to listen, but I was also responding with caring criticism, honesty, and affirmation of their work.

LESSON #1 – Student-Generated Topics Should Shape Curriculum

In the second week of class, I asked students to begin writing about what they see in the school. Immediately, students began talking about what they feel and how their teachers are problematic for them. Prior to having them spend a few weeks capturing details of the school, I framed a week-long conversation about teachers. I began with a freewrite that responded to the one word on the board: school. Most students wrote about offensive and irrelevant teachers, telling stories that would have been hilarious if not for the sheer volume of negativity. I turned this discussion into two interrelated lessons: the first was a math lesson and the second was a lesson on defining vague terms in solid detail. Both of these lessons were framed around students generating the content of our course, and around ensuring students understood the gravity of what they were saying. Thus these interrelated lessons aimed to validate student experiences and knowledge, while framing curriculum.

The following day, we addressed, in a quick math lesson, how many "good" teachers these students had previously experienced prior to their current school. I asked how many teachers had the entire class been exposed to, and what percentage of that total number were "good" teachers. Each student wrote down their list of "good" teachers, yet in a class of twenty students, only three total teachers were identified as "good." Students then estimated the number of teachers they had at their many schools, and then multiplied that by the number of students in our class. It was a powerful lesson for me as well: students averaged twelve teachers for Kindergarten through sixth grade, fourteen teachers for 7th and 8th grades, and twenty teachers for 9th and 10th grade, for a total of forty-six teachers per student. On the board, two students mapped out our discussion in numeric terms:

1) 20 students x 46 teachers = 920 total teachers

2) 3 "good" teachers (out of 920 teachers)
      3 divided by 920 = .3% of teachers were "good"

Students discussed which number accurately captured how few of their previous teachers were good, and decided that three out of 920 teachers sounded worse than .3%. We spent the rest of the period creatively writing about the paltry number of "good" teachers students had.

The following day centered on breaking down what we had just done: I pushed the class to define exactly what makes a teacher "good" and several linked what we had done to standardized tests in math. Lucinda clarified: "The math only made sense because we had conversations to make sense of numbers. But the math on [standardized] tests don't give no context." I then pushed beyond the numbers to clarify what "good" meant according to each of them. Many students disagreed with whether or not a rigid teacher or a more laid-back teacher was good, and the class began to dive into descriptions based on personal experience. They all agreed that, as Raquel stated: "Good teachers care about us." I pushed for further clarification by asking how a good teacher lets students know they are cared for. The class generated a quick list that I jotted down during class:

Things A Teacher Does To Care:
      1. Ask about and remember us
      2. Know how to calm me down
      3. Know how to calm my friends down
      4. Be themselves

5. *Does not get angry at me*
6. *Does not take bullshit from other students*
7. *Does not take bullshit from other teachers or the principal*
8. *Knows when I come to the class bleeding on the inside*
9. *Trusts us!*

Students then wrote additional freewrites about each of these nine points, storytelling with concrete examples of when teachers demonstrated their care. While the students created a powerful list of qualities that make a teacher "good," very few teachers receive any sort of training on this list. No Child Left Behind's definition of highly qualified teacher does not include teachers "being themselves" or anger management, and while the focus on knowing students may be abstract, many educators have long argued for ensuring teachers care and know their students (Gay, 1994; Noddings, 1984; Palmer, 1998).[4]

I engaged students in a culminating conversation to think about how school structures could help teachers care more. The purpose was to help students see an end point to their initiated conversation, but also that their insights could lead directly to policy outcomes. The conversation lasted two days, and centered initially on pushing "bad" teachers. Ermalinda argued that, in addition to caring, teachers should be held accountable for student learning, such that "if we are failed for getting 50% of the questions right, shouldn't educators be fired if only 50% of us graduate?" Other students chimed in by arguing for measurements that impact teacher salary (including graduation rates, whether teachers are liked by students, and whether teachers engage in their communities). Towards the end of the conversation, students began to argue that even if teachers are beholden to standardized curriculum, they could be caring by noticing them, and that should be noted in their evaluations. Marcus clarified this: "The teachers teach the same boring stuff, but they also notice if I don't show up, and that means a lot." The lesson concluded with students wrestling with how they could evaluate teacher effectiveness and care, and with them thinking a bit more about what that could look like as school policy.

---

4   Yet despite that some of these texts are used in teacher education programs across the country, it is important to assess if and how teachers learn to be caring and knowing of all students, particularly given that teacher effectiveness is increasingly measured by student scores on standardized tests (Darling-Hammond & Berry, 2006).

LESSON #2 – Responsive Educators Identify and Respond to Anger

Roughly one month into the semester, one student read her freewrite aloud, capturing her vision of the inside of juvenile hall. She triggered an intense discussion, and I asked students to share their experiences: two-thirds of the class had spent anywhere from one night to nine months in youth facilities. The room was loud as anxious voices shared stories of being physically abused by guards, of hearing "blood dripping onto cold concrete floors," of hearing "shouts from a room next door when another kid hung herself." An almost surreal eagerness to share negative experiences permeated the room. I told the class I was overwhelmed by how much they had experienced, by their expertise and insight, and of their ability to share in public such traumatic experiences. I reminded them that they had direct insight and knowledge about a system that many of their teachers knew very little about. As the class filtered out, I noticed a shift in our community; students were serious, somber, but also gave each other a bit more shared respect.

A week later, I facilitated a student-initiated discussion that began with prisons, and shifted to police brutality. Most students shared stories where they had been disrespected or abused by police officers within the past six months. Everyone had a friend or family member who had recent violent experiences with local police. The atmosphere was tense: students shared experiences that triggered student rage at being mistreated, at seeing those they loved being mistreated by formal societal structures they felt they could do nothing about. In addition, Oakland police had just shot and killed Gary King, a local resident many of the students knew (Rayburn, 2000). I had been pushing students to clarify in concrete details when they said, "I was beat," or "They messed me up." All of a sudden, Michael angrily swiped the top of his desk clean: his journal, sheets of paper, and a pencil flew across the room. The class immediately stopped, and everyone stared at Michael, waiting. Seemingly oblivious, he put his headphones on and blasted hip hop, making any further conversation difficult. The class tried to continue the conversation, raising voices to be heard over his obvious anger. I wrote the following immediately after class:

> *His rage seething to the beat*
> *Head phones bump bump blam*
> *All the class hears is Curse Bitch Fuck Damn*
>
> *Does not look up when*
> *I call his name*
> *Not even the third time*

I crowd around his desk
Say his name again
Dance around eke out a smile
Or laughter to release closed tight fists

His rage sends heat waves across the class
The loud hum of the air-conditioner kicks on
His eyes do not move
Do not acknowledge me 18 inches from his face

He had been engaged in the conversation
Listening as student after student
Relayed stories of police brutality
Young bodies slammed against colonial concrete

And perhaps he heard one too many stories
Perhaps one more story triggered the rage
Of police fists batons bullets aimed at his people
Or maybe his family
Or maybe his body

Or perhaps he just shut off
At the rage others felt

What I do know
His rage
Erupted and he placed his rage
Squarely in the hip music hop
That allowed him to remain
In class
Full of loud rage
Not violent

What I do know
Is this is not on
A standardized test.

The following day, I asked Michael to read my words silently before beginning class, and asked him how he'd like to conduct class. After reading, he put his fist to his heart, grinned at me, and suggested I take the class from there. After a class discussion on what works to deescalate intense situations, he thanked me and told me he'd write a response tomorrow. I asked him how he felt and he replied "right on, good." He asked how I knew, and looked me in the eye for several moments, measuring my intent. He did not want what I wrote read aloud to the class, but my validating his unspoken rage did something profound for Michael. He knew that I knew why he was angry. After class, he came up to me and said that "having you know means a lot cause no one notices." His attendance and writing presence skyrocketed after this experience, and that day he wrote in his after school journal:

> From what you wrote about me yesterday was kinda trust. I did have
> this big rage. Mad at the world and really didn't care to hear too
> many more police stories. Once people start to talk about the times
> when the police harras or did some to them, maybe it was one too
> many story's and that's so true. The music was slappin, "Solider
> boy, in watch me, crank that solider boy that super man the O."
> The words of the song I really don't understand but the beat kept my
> listening…

My reaching out to acknowledge his rage was risky; Michael could have rejected my poetic approach and shut down even further. I likely would have lost his respect had I been wrong about his anger. Yet instead, he met my challenge and increased engagement partially because he knew that, at least in our class, there was less reason to hide what he felt. But he also demonstrated how his outlet, while it may have worked this time, was not meeting his goal of reducing rage. He thus opened up for conversation for to continue by writing: "the words of the song I really don't understand." I began using music in the classroom that focused on rage, and without directly addressing Michael, had the class wrestle with music as an escape from rage-evoking situations.

LESSON #3 – Trauma is Relevant and Academic

Two months into the school year, Raquel shared her voice. I had just written a two-page response to her in-class and out-of-class journals, which had moved me with her rage-filled honest attempts at capturing her world. In my response, I urged her to clarify with more concrete details. The next day, her typically bold voice shook for the first time, despite reading aloud daily. She expressed her pain: "I have been molested.

I repeat this so you cannot deny me: I have been molested." Raquel went into details; what her cousins did to her, what her mother did to her, things no one protected her from. She talked about how teachers always seemed afraid to ask how she was really feeling: "they'd ask and walk on, not waiting for a response." Raquel captured specific experiences in precise language as she shared pieces of her story. She expressed the pain of seeing her mother abused and demonstrated the mental instability such violence causes. She argued that she had "no foundation to love."

After reading her four pages aloud, the class erupted into applause. Students congratulated her, told her she was brave, and thanked her for trusting the class. I asked her how she felt: "my hands are still shaking," she replied, "but really good. Thank you all for listening. I've been needing to get that off my chest." When I asked for how long, she replied, "since birth." The conversation ended a few minutes after the usual class-scattering bell when Lucinda remarked: "Damn, Chris, school should be like this all the time."

While the class had been sharing "voice" and reflecting on traumatic events in their lives and community, violence was largely being framed as something that happened to others (with prison and police encounters being the one exception). Students were writing to me and expressing their explicit experiences with violence, but had yet to break the ice of public sharing of more difficult to share pain. After Raquel broke that barrier, the class began to shift, and students increasingly shared glimpses into the intense emotional trauma many of them were living. While we edited to ensure our points were clarified, we also spent entire class sessions on one or two students' pressing trauma. Raquel clarified the impact such focus had on the classroom community: "Now that I know about José and Tanie and Michael, I feel more safe sharing, too. Actually, I feel like I should because they did. If I want us to be close, I should also be exposed."

Often, students used freewrites to expand upon trauma they wrote about in their at-home journals, and were moved to read such emotionally heavy experiences aloud. On those days, I'd ask the student if they wanted us to come back to their work after others shared. I did this as a way to bring the entire class' focus on one student, but also to ensure adequate focus on intense issues that could trigger other students' emotional responses.[5] I tried to provide closure to our conversations by reminding students that sharing voice is emotional work. I also demonstrated how thick details that capture oppression helps develop a foundation of solid, needed writing. This expression also enhances student articulation, as they receive critical feedback and learn to speak aloud to audiences that may be hostile.

Tanie began coming to class midway through the semester because her writing class was "boring and the teacher disrespects me." Tanie continued to ditch her other class until I convinced her other teacher to let her enroll in our class. After two weeks in our class, she read aloud a poem about being raped at a party. The class was silent for about thirty seconds afterwards, and I asked her to re-read the poem to make sure everyone heard her in the way she wanted to be heard. After finishing the second time, another student stated simply: "Let's talk about being raped." After a few minutes of almost total silence (incredibly rare in high school classes, but particularly our class), a few other students agreed, and soon the entire class said they wanted to discuss rape.

What followed was one of our most engaging conversations. After I reiterated our expectations that anyone disrespecting or denying anyone else's experiences would not be allowed back in the class, students dove in. Students shared being molested, raped, assaulted, and their survival through family violence; afterwards, several students would stand up, ask the student if they wanted a hug, and sit in shared silence. Then another student would join in the sharing, until almost everyone in the class shared their personal connections to living through sexualized violence. Students validated each other, and were helping each other develop a language to talk about violence that is often seen as shameful. It also marked a rare instance where men shared their experiences of molestation. Most students wrote about how they needed that conversation in their journals, and many talked to me individually afterwards, thanking me for the conversation they initiated (and created the safe conditions for).

---

5   I was also clear that what students shared was confidential. I reserved the right to have follow-up conversation with all students to ensure their safety, and often used my feedback as a way to extend one-on-one conversations and suggest resources. Creating the safety to have these conversations required that students not be threatened by my reporting their trauma to an adult they did not trust: most shared repeated experiences with counselors and law enforcement personnel who punished them for sharing trauma. Thus, they did not trust most professional adults, and stated that they would not have worked to develop voice had I enforced upon them interactions with school or district counselors. As such, I referred most students to an off-campus free counseling service where they could share their trauma in a confidential setting.

I shared what I wrote that evening with the class the following day:

her voice timid she re-read the poem
and now her voice strong, she became the
character in the poem
the young girl raped in the bathroom
molested at 7 years
she owned the class with her pain
and tears we all shared
stories of survival and the loneliness
of family rejection
wounds upon wounds
and seven young women spoke of being molested
even two young men shared (finally, terribly)
their shared inability to stop memory

as i left the school, i heard Michael
on his cell phone
clarifying between rape and molestation
initiating a conversation with someone he loves
loving a conversation into the phone
and once again
i'm reminded that standardized tests and
plot-graphs are simply not the most important
or slightly relevant chains shaping these
students
our future.

Upon hearing me, students launched into a discussion about how they would learn more if school helped them with what they needed to overcome. "We are looking for answers, but mostly, we can't ask questions or we get sent to the principal's office," argued Raquel. These students were seeking answers to the impossible dilemmas they face, and their teachers are ill-equipped to provide answers. And they were beginning to create space for wrestling with trauma they knew they had to address. Michael had ongoing conversation with a woman he loved about the pain she felt from being sexually abused. But he did not know how to talk to his friend, and the class helped him understand the impact of sexual abuse, but also his role in helping provide support. Michael applied what he had just learned from an incredibly risky conversation, and had been able to (finally) get his questions answered by women that he was uncomfortable initiating such a conversation with.

LESSON #4 – Engaged Students Rarely Drop Out

Mid-way through the semester, I had several conversations with other teachers who expressed frustration that attendance had dropped; less than half of the students were regularly attending school. Yet our classroom was often full, with only a few students absent per day. Indeed, many students began coming to school only for our class, and expressed this repeatedly during our class, honoring their peers and me by letting us know they only came for us. Due to the clear disparities between attendance rates in our class and other classes, I urged students to think about what brought them to our class (and conversely, what kept them from attending their other courses). My intent was to increase attendance rates across the board, since attending our class alone would not increase their chances at graduating.

One student clarified what would bring her peers to class: "Give us a reason to come to school and we will." When asked what would bring them to school, the class wrote a list on the board that included:

1) *daily skills relevant to our survival*
2) *self defense*
3) *anger management*
4) *drug and alcohol counseling*
5) *respect for us and our families*
6) *provide a safe place for us to learn*
7) *nice teachers*
8) *good books*
9) *include us regardless of the languages we speak*

This list reflects the immediate circumstances that shape student lives and demonstrates how they are interested in managing these issues. These students were reflecting on what they needed, and in so doing, were also identifying how problematic their realities were. The contrast between our class and their other classes seemed to be growing, as our class was increasingly a source of support and personal challenge, whereas other courses tended to stick to standardized curriculum, even if the teachers were caring. Thus, students wanted teaching methods and approaches that reflected their context, and began to demand individualized recognition. I was deeply troubled by this shift. While I wanted students to focus on their own healing, I was not sure how to get the class to recognize the value of academics, even if school did not reflect their needs.

Students wanted safe spaces to be themselves, to temporarily let down their guards to make sense of the reality they live in, assess the effectiveness of their survival strategies, and make changes in their daily actions to achieve the goals they set out for themselves. One student, Ermalinda, clarified the need for schools to not perpetuate what they live at home: "I get enough violence and argument at home. I don't need more of that in school." Yet students felt school presented the same violence, silencing, and dismissal they received at home and their surrounding community, despite positive intentions from their educators and peers.

José clarified what academic failure meant to him:

> Listen, if I fail a test that asks me questions I have never seen, that judges me based on courses I did not take, is that my fault? Is it my responsibility to learn what a teacher don't teach? If so, then give me my rights as an adult. But if not, then don't test me on things I don't know. I can tell you what I don't know without having to sit through your test. But let me ask teachers this: Can you survive on my block? Can you raise two children, work 30 hours a week, take care of a dying mother with cancer, and avoid getting jumped in my neighborhood? Cause to fail at that means to die.

What I tried to do was shift the conversation from cynical critique into one of self-empowerment and motivation. These students were increasingly expressive of their critical thinking and observations. They were reading (a little). They were writing (a lot). But they were not doing much work in their other classes (if they attended them at all). Relying upon critical race theory, I shifted up the class focus, and provided more perspectives on navigating barriers in order to directly challenge them. Guest speakers like comedian W. Kamau Bell talked about making a living off of critical expression, and that such a living required "continual efforts to work, to learn, to understand what makes the world so messed up." Students watched documentaries about enslaved children in Africa and made comparisons to local urban communities. While I kept up our freewriting and voice-centeredness, I shifted the curriculum to reflect what I saw as a need to keep students engaged in larger conversations about equity, racism, and their personal need to engage deeply in navigating the problematic but very real hoops in front of them.

A dramatic shift came when our class was visited by two musicians from Zimbabwe (Oliver Mtukudzi and Sam Mataure). Students had already written responses to several of their songs, and watched a short documentary on the band (The Black Spirits). We followed that with analysis of what the lyrics meant; focusing on language and storytelling to preserve memory and history, and to ensure violence is talked about openly. When Oliver Mtukudzi and Sam Mataure visited the class, much of the school community joined in on the conversation, eager to welcome our international guests. The discussion helped the class reflect on the universal nature of Black struggle, but also on the importance of doing work to help the community. Oliver Mtukudzi argued that "young people have to work to better yourself so that you can better the community." He continued that "in Zimbabwe, if people do not have something to say, we do not let them," meaning that in order to speak, you have to have something to say.

The visit was powerful; students wrote letters to Oliver Mtukudzi thanking him for preserving culture and music through singing in Shona and talked about how they had never before had access to an African elder. Rather than critique the shortcomings in their schooling, however, the students were shifting already, and began praising him for his efforts. As students increasingly requested his music (which dramatically differs from the fast paced hip hop they are used to), they also began to hear his message: critique is essential, but has to be expressed in a way that a wide audience can hear. His method is music, but his point was heard by many of the students: they would have to engage much more deeply, and not just in our class, if they were to live as they wanted to, and shape the world as they dreamed.

LESSON #5 – Engaged Educators Trust Students

Towards the end of the semester, I gave students an intentionally vague freewrite on the prompt "It Happened." My point on avoiding vague words like 'it' and 'happened' had been made repeatedly, so students knew I was asking them to write whatever they wanted. Almost every student chose a powerful, personal topic, and many wrote their most engaging, detailed piece. I asked students how this assignment engaged them, and most responded that they knew I was "messing" with them because they knew I "hated those two words." They also felt like I knew them because I trusted them enough to work out what Tanie called "a vague ass assignment." In framing an assignment as playful, I gave students space to show what they had learned, and most students jumped at a chance to express their reality, in their voice. Listen to Lucinda's example:

It Happened
I believed another lie
another line another black man
shouldn't have been my boyfriend
thinking my open legs would save him from lock up

It Happened
I believed my father despite
another time another brown man
I knew he could walk out this time I knew his fist
thinking my quiet would save my mom

It Happened
I believed my 8th grade counselor
another line another white man
he told me I was beautiful then made me take my clothes off
thinking I'd be dead soon anyhow

It Happened
I believed my mother's brother
another time another yellow man
he told me to shut up or die
thinking my bedroom was safe for his sick

It Happened
I young girl soon woman
woke up wanting more
still don't say no but now I know
thinking my life might just be worth.

Lucinda's poem demonstrates that how assignments are framed matters. This assignment told students that I wanted to see their clarity, but I did not have to tell them that explicitly. Having already clarified the importance of not being vague through avoiding such words (it, happened, good, bad, stuff, something, interesting), I encouraged students to dance with whatever words they wanted so long as they were clear. This would not have happened if I did not lay out the structures ahead of time, if I did not continually remind students that, for example, 'racism' is a vague term that does not capture what they live, think, and feel. I did not tell Lucinda to write about the violent sexism in her life, but she used the assignment to wrestle with issues she faces daily.

Students ended up reading this assignment aloud in class, at a school-wide forum, and at open mic performances because most students felt proud of work they initiated, and because they framed the entire topic of conversation, with no instructional expectations.

Lucinda also demonstrated that when critical race theory is applied to the classroom, educators must follow-up with each individual student. Because she referred to intense emotional experiences without prompting, my responsibility was to provide direct feedback in the form of personal, critical writing. And I did this throughout the course; as students wrote more about their own struggles, I shared with them my insight and personal struggles in letters written directly to them. I also offered up counseling support through a free public service, because students repeatedly indicated that they did not trust district counselors. And through such written and spoken dialogue, the course grew together in our shared understandings that without acknowledging and expressing how concretely oppression impacts us, we will simply repeat the cycles of violence that most of us live.

Responsive Teaching

What teachers need to know most is this: stop making me do stupid shit! I get shot at. Cops fuck with me. I have no real home. So let me blow up creatively.

- Freddie

Because my experiences as a student shape my insight as an educator, I share my growing up years with current students. As a student, I spent hours waiting for the principal, who yelled at me to stop being a disturbance, before giving me a packet of worksheets for classes I was not enrolled in. I was required to meet weekly with interchangeable school counselors "because I was angry," and my required counselors gave me articles about anger (but since I did not do my homework, I obviously did not do their homework). I remember multiple counselors pleading for me to calm down, but no one ever asked if I was being beat by my father. No one ever asked if I was being molested. None of my educators gave me the space to talk about what I was reacting to. In essence, I was disciplined rather than taught how to deal with my pain. As a poor white student, and as an educator in rural, suburban, and urban schools for over a decade, I have come to see school as designed to keep personal experiences as far outside the classroom as possible.

Freddie reminded me of seventh grade; he rarely attended school and in one seven week stretch, came only four days. When he did come, he told me he was often "told to sit quietly and do worksheets." What incentive, he asked me, does he have to attend school that he sees as well-intentioned, but irrelevant? "I like the teachers here," he clarified, "but they don't live the bullshit I do. And they teach me to go to college. Which I need. But that does not help me get home alive. And it don't help my addictions." Freddie left me angry about the use of standardized tests to measure abilities that are simply irrelevant at this stage in his life. Knowing how to express math and English in standardized ways may be important, but not compared to Freddie's pressing need to dodge real life-taking bullets. "Algebra don't compare to mama's rent money, commas and periods don't raise my baby brothers who be home after school today, tomorrow, yesterday."

These students were simply not concerned with standardized math and English skill measurements. While economic and social mobility were tangible goals for these students, the things they need to do to survive each day created barriers to economic mobility. They noticed that their educators have not valued the skills that keep students alive. They noticed that they scored poorly on standardized tests that ignore the tangible conflict negotiation skills they use to arrive at school daily. Students continually complained that their other classes had nice teachers, but were teaching things that would not help them in their immediate needs. My urging them to work both towards the future by jumping seemingly irrelevant academic hoops while simultaneously developing real world survival skills often was ignored because they were, as Raquel stated angrily: "com-fucking-pletely over-fucking-whelmed just trying to fucking survive each day." Our class then continually returned to capturing the everyday as a way to 1) develop and express voice as a way of releasing stress; 2) demonstrate the overwhelming nature of racism, poverty, and violence that shapes everyday life; and 3) develop the tools to survive.

Lupe, an undergraduate student who assisted with the course, argued that "students do not value the types of knowledge they need to learn to do well" on standardized tests, and the students were clear that this is partially because those types of knowledge deny how they exist. Listening to students exposes this clashing of values that must be addressed if students are to be engaged in school. These students realized the futility of knowledge unrelated to their sheer survival; this is what they most often wrote about. Listening and validating voice shows students that they too can create knowledge, but also that they already have a solid foundation from which to build. As Geneva Gay (2000), argued in *Culturally Responsive Teaching*, "while school failure is an *experience* of too many ethnically diverse students, it is not the *identity* of any."

Conclusion: Shifting Toward Student Voices

My purpose as an educator is to counter the penalization many students of color expect when they speak with passion. But my attempts also partially set students up to fail because they will be punished for speaking their minds, in future classrooms and across society. Yet they should not be punished in a democracy for speaking their experiences, and it is towards that aim that I encourage expression. Yet as critical, outspoken students of color, they know well their chances for economic mobility decrease with their outspokenness. They have heard about Malcolm X and Dr. King's assassinations, but have also survived dozens of real assassinations on their blocks. The seemingly all-out-war they live in has more relevance than the fear of speaking out, but they also recognize what appears to be the futility of speaking out: they often ask "if no one hears you, what is the point of speaking out?" That is the weakness of applying critical race theory to only one class or only one school: educators cannot require anyone to listen to these students. But educators can share tools to express ourselves without fear, knowing we may be penalized, but that voice is too important to silence. Structurally, that is what critical race theory's application to education requires: to no longer penalize students for speaking their realities, and to instead shift reality by demanding that all voices be included, particularly voices that are silenced by the structures of oppression.

Applying critical race theory creates such spaces, particularly for students of color and low income white students. It is with such a framework that I argue the U.S. educational system needs to be entirely re-envisioned. Applied critical race theory exposes racism within a core curriculum that enhances storytelling about who we are and how we live. And while I center race in my framing of critical race theory, because I also employ culturally responsive approaches, gender, sexuality, class, ability, and family structures are also centered in my teaching. Thus, applied critical race theory, connected to culturally responsiveness, is an entry way into redeveloping the system of education towards an equitable, community-centered, democratic process of creating a sustained country of hope. Applied critical race theorist/practitioners begin with race as a foundation to center voice that illuminates realties for people of color, women, gays, lesbians, bisexuals, transgendered people, people with disabilities, all faith-based communities, poor communities, and folks of all body types, shades, and shapes.

I teach passionately because my educational experiences were largely dry, redundant, disrespectful, and white male supremacist. I try to be myself in the classroom because I never had a white teacher that made it okay to be who I am, with my own personal histories of violent abuse and neglect. Through coming to express my voice, I began to witness how others lived similar lives, and came to realize that I am a survivor of genocide, family violence, poverty, and schools designed to silence my voice about all of these. This is the purpose of developing voice: to have students develop confidence in our lives, in the idea that we may not be able to change society overnight, but we can identify and alter our personal reactions now.

Chapter 11

The Role of Inquiry in Teacher Leadership: Examining Student Achievement in Multicultural Settings

by Barbara A. Storms and Gloria M. Rodriguez

Because schools are social organizations where no one person (not any one teacher or one administrator) can implement systemic change, making progress on core issues necessitates group understanding and exploration of topics.

Barbara Storms

Teacher-Led Collaborative Inquiry

Inquiry, often described as questioning about or exploring issues, can be a powerful process for school reform. It can be a tool for improving communication among and between staff. It can provide processes for surfacing, investigating, and talking about difficult issues. Inquiry can also be a vehicle for developing and putting action plans into place. Often the culture in schools focuses on "doing." This translates into "do" identify a problem, "do" create solutions to address that problem, then "do" move on to the next problem. This tendency to "just do it" – to jump into action without taking time to develop an understanding of the complexity of issues or to set a clear course of action--does not result in lasting change. While the urgency to improve schools is real, and the accountability pressures are many, this "do-do-do" process does little to ensure that core issues and various perspectives about those issues are systematically explored. In inquiry, time and effort spent in clarifying a topic and identifying a course to follow generally ensure more success in creating meaningful actions to address issues.

Inquiry is local research. It is formative. It is informal in many senses. While No Child Left Behind (NCLB) emphasizes scientific research, actually setting up control group studies in schools is seldom feasible or even reasonable. And yet, the information that is most publicized these days--standardized testing results--gives little direction for curricular or instructional changes. Therefore, working to identify more immediate sources of local information (e.g., student work, review and observation of lessons, feedback from students, parents and teachers) to help guide improvement efforts is a reasonable step in on-going change efforts. Inquiry provides a structure for defining topics, setting our questions to explore, collecting and analyzing information, in order to create action plans that then define the next cycle of questions, data collection, and analysis and action adjustments (e.g., Anderson, Herr, & Nihlen, 1994; Kailin, 1999; Newman, 2005).

Background

The insights presented in this chapter grow out of the authors' work of coaching over 125 teachers who led school-based, collaborative inquiry processes which, while focusing on school improvement, also met the requirements of a master's degree program (Lee, Storms, Camp & Bronzini, 2002; Lee & Storms, 1999; Storms & Lee, in press). Most of these teachers worked in urban, multicultural settings where the pressure to improve the academic performance of students of color is real and immediate. Many of the teachers with whom we have worked found inquiry to be not only useful to them for improving their instructional practices, but also for developing knowledge and skills that enhanced their roles as leaders in their schools.

Why Collaboration Matters

Because schools are social organizations where no one person (not any one teacher or any one administrator) can implement systemic change, making progress on core issues necessitates group understanding and exploration of topics. Seldom is an issue defined in the same way by all persons or groups (e.g., teachers, staff, parents) at a school. Together a group at a school can develop a common way of defining an issue and from that definition then begin to coordinate efforts to examine it. Collaborative inquiry builds on teacher professionalism and breaks down teacher isolation that too often works against innovation and meaningful change (Darling-Hammond, 1995; Little, 1990).

The collaborative nature of inquiry, and its focus on group "sense making," (Garmston & Wellman, 1999; Sergiovanni, 1992; Weick, 1995), helps to ensure that multiple perspectives about issues are considered. This is important because the context of a school site matters. While issues may be similar at various schools, the ways in which issues manifest themselves differ by context. Important foundational work for inquiry includes building a collaborative group to explore how an issue is defined and played out at a school.

We believe that teachers are well-positioned to lead these inquiry and school improvement efforts. Teachers are the "front line" in learning. They are the ones who design and enact the student interactions that can improve learning. When teachers come together in inquiry efforts, they support the definitions of teacher leadership that emphasize relationships and collaboration in-group efforts (Gonzales & Lambert, 2001;Yorks-Barr & Duke, 2004).

Examples of Inquiry & Teacher Leadership

Teachers are the heart of the educational system and, as such, touch all levels of school districts from individual classrooms to school-wide and district programs. At the classroom level, most often teachers involved in inquiry center those efforts on teaching and learning, which are so very closely linked. For classroom teachers investigating their teaching practices or studying how students in their classrooms are learning is the very essence of the teachers' work. Many teachers use inquiry as a process for developing, implementing or evaluating school level or district programs. The following are examples of how teachers at various levels of school districts lead inquiry efforts that centered on student achievement, particularly improving the achievement of students of color. These examples are indicative of the types of inquiries that we have coached teachers to lead.

Classroom Level Inquiry

Using inquiry at the classroom level to investigate how students learn or how to improve that learning is not new. Many teachers have written about these efforts and many scholars have studied them (Yorks-Barr & Duke, 2004). However, because the teachers we work with are training to become leaders in schools, and because we required them to engage in collaborative inquiry, classroom teachers in our programs had to look outside their own individual classrooms to involve other teachers, staff, students, and parents in their inquiry efforts. Recently, many school districts in California have adopted reading and language arts programs that claim to be linked to the state standards assessment. For many teachers, especially those in schools with large bilingual or English language learner (ELL) populations, these adoptions can raise many questions as some have limited materials for students whose home language is other than English.

One teacher in such a school with a large ELL population, Juan, was not only worried about the many English Language Learners in his classroom and whether the new language arts program would help them improve their language skills, but he was also interested in how the other teachers at his grade level would implement the new language arts program for the first time. Within a school schedule that allowed for one afternoon of meeting time a week, two of these afternoons each month were set aside for grade level meetings. Juan encouraged his fourth grade level team early on in the school year, rather than talking about class activities, to begin to lay out questions that teachers had about the new adoption in relation to their students' achievement. Teachers noted that although they had some training in the new program, the complexity of teaching new lessons and using materials for the first time concerned them. Also, because the state tests weren't given until nearly the end of the school year and results weren't available until the next fall, teachers were very concerned about using diagnostic assessments to help them adjust their lessons to meet their current student needs.

These fourth grade teachers agreed to try out lessons and bring back lesson plans, reflect on those lessons, and select samples of student work including teacher-developed assessments to share with their colleagues on a biweekly basis. As the year progressed, the fourth grade teachers observed each other's teaching. They also looked together at unit assessments to determine how students were doing, paying special attention to English language learners who had been the lowest performing group on their campus. By the end of the year, they found that inadequate training had greatly affected the way in which teachers used the program. Teachers were discouraged because while English language learners did make some progress, they continued to struggle with language development. The teachers working together found that using inquiry allowed them to monitor the students' performance and alter activities along the way even though they felt the outcomes improved only slightly.

The collegiality and sharing that inquiry required pushed teachers to question their own teaching practices in terms of student performance. Juan took the lead in the inquiry by organizing the agendas for the meetings and keeping track of group agreements, questions, and lessons learned. He also led the group effort at the end of the school year to develop a presentation to share with other teachers about what the fourth grade teachers had learned. They not only presented to the current teaching staff at the end of that school year, but they also expected to use the presentation if any new fourth grade teachers joined their school the next year.

Program Level Inquiry

Even before NCLB required that schools offer after-school programs, many schools had already developed interventions for students who were not achieving. In a number of schools, the focus of these intervention efforts was on designing, implementing, and staffing such programs, not on determining whether they were improving student achievement. Teacher-led inquiry proved to be a powerful strategy for determining what was working and not working in this intervention evaluation sample.

King Elementary School, like many schools in the larger San Francisco Bay Area, has a very diverse student population. Several years before, a group of teachers designed and implemented an after-school program for students in the third grade who were falling behind in class. Generally, the students were failing one or more subject(s); some had been held back a year in school. The after-school program was intended to give students small group instruction that would bring them to grade level in reading and math.

One of the teachers, Victoria, who had been teaching third grade at the school for several years and who had also taught in the after-school program, decided to engage her peers in assessing the success of the program. The other third grade teachers happily joined Victoria in reviewing the state test scores in reading and math for students who had been in the intervention over the previous two years. They were convinced that they would see improvements in the test scores for the intervention students; however, the results showed little change from one year to the next.

Fueled by the apparent lack of improvement, the group decided to lay out their assumptions about the students who were generally identified for intervention. The student group identified in any given year was approximately 50% African American and 50% Latino, even though there were other ethnic groups at the school. The teachers assumed that most of the African American students in the intervention moved around a lot and transferred into the school fairly recently. Using school enrollment information, they found that most of the African American students in the intervention had attended King since kindergarten. The teachers also assumed that most of the Latino students were English language learners when, in fact, more than 75% of the Latino students were classified as English proficient, and most of the Latino students also had been at the school since kindergarten.

Surprised on all counts—who the students were, what their backgrounds were and what the testing results were—the teachers decided to look more closely at the after-school program. Much of what was taught was not reflected in the third grade standards, those on which the students would be tested in the state test at the end of that school year; instead much of the emphasis of the third grade intervention program was on skills from the second or first grade standards. The teachers also found that there was little connection between what was being tested in the after-school program and what the state test assessed. These revelations helped teachers understand why the labor intensive, after-school effort had garnered few positive academic results for students. As the year progressed, the group completed a comprehensive review of the program, designing and implementing changes from how students were identified, to the content and design of the delivery, and the on-going assessment throughout. In addition to revising the intervention program, the group presented their findings to their peers.

Victoria led the group by often gathering materials (such as test results and sample assessments) that the group would use in their discussions. She also kept track of "ah-ha's" and questions the group wanted to revisit. Throughout the year, she documented agreements and kept track of changes in the program. The inquiry findings showed that on-going work around program evaluation needed to be used to monitor the success of the teachers' (and students') efforts. In future years, the group would refer to these notes as they continued the process of determining how and in what way their efforts were meeting the current needs of students.

System Level Inquiry

In both of the previous examples, teachers led inquiry efforts with other teachers to examine teaching and learning, at the classroom and program levels. In both of these cases, the school administration supported the teacher inquiry efforts. At times, however, classroom and school level changes are not enough. To bring about lasting improvements, work must be done at the system level. And while some classroom teachers may believe that they have little influence on the system (e.g., district, county) in which they work, other teachers have found ways to leverage their classroom perspective in system-level change efforts (Brynjulson & Storms, 2005). Sometimes, this work occurs as classroom teachers serve on district committees. At other times, as in the example below, teachers take on special assignments at a district level where they are not administrators but have access to administrators across schools. Reforming school systems so that they support effective instruction for all students is challenging yet important work that teachers can lead successfully.

As a teacher on special assignment working with new teachers, Maria heard the frustrations of teachers who felt ill-equipped to work with all of the cultures represented in their classrooms. She also heard from school principals who were concerned with how well the students of color in their schools were performing. She used the time at the end of a district meeting to identify principals who wanted to discuss student achievement with other principals. With the support of her supervisor, Maria set up a meeting with the self-identified principals. Prior to the meeting, she worked with the district's data services to retrieve state testing results for the past three years for each of the principals' schools, disaggregated by ethnicity and grade level. When the principals met, they shared their concerns about how students of color were falling behind at their schools. Armed with the assessment data, the group found that this assumption was both true and not true: African American students, as a group, were the least successful students on the state assessment, but other ethnic groups were making progress, even if they were not yet at the level of achievement of the White students. The group decided to focus on the achievement of African American students during this school year. They agreed to read the latest research about African American student achievement, interview African American students, and survey the parents of these students.

Maria's role was vital to the group's success. She searched out recent research and brought it to the group for discussion. She found surveys from published research that the group reviewed and revised for their own use. She developed drafts of interview questions (and permission forms) and worked with the research department and the principals to hone the drafts that they used. The completed surveys were sent to her attention at the district. She interviewed students and collected the comments that the principals gathered in the interviews they conducted. She then organized the data and took it back to the group. Because of Maria's efforts, the group could keep on track and move forward during the year. Once the principals, Maria, and other district administrators (who asked to join the group) analyzed the results, they found that African American students and parents believed that teachers generally expected less of them academically than teachers did of other students. The group agreed that much work needed to be done to help the predominately White teaching staff come to terms with their stereotypes about African American students and also to increase academic expectations for and assistance to these students. The outcome of this work was a presentation to all of the principals and district leaders and an action plan for continuing to explore student achievement the next school year.

Teachers Leading for Equity in a Context of High Stakes Accountability

Major news services continue to report that public schools are failing to provide many students, particularly students of color, a quality education. Recent school reform initiatives at the local, state, and national levels are driven, in part, by public demands for schools to demonstrate success in teaching an increasingly diverse population of students. Under No Child Left Behind (NCLB, 2001), the pressure on schools to improve achievement has become very public as school and district rankings and test scores are publicized in newspapers and on web sites. Easy access to school testing results ensures that the public can compare school performance data. While there are many reasons for educators to lament the increased spotlight on test scores and other measures under NCLB, and to question the intense pressure being applied, based on the limited information that standardized tests give (Popham, 1999, 2001), there are others in education who view this as an opportunity to engage actively with others at their schools on the issues of equity of outcomes for students. We must then consider this question: How do we ensure that all students in our increasingly diverse population are prepared to be successful in a rapidly changing and increasingly technological American society? More importantly, what can be done to guarantee that all students achieve to their fullest potential? Obviously, there are no simple answers to these questions. However, we are finding that teachers who use inquiry as a way to explore their practice and the achievement of their students find it to be a powerful tool for reform.

Our experiences of working with teachers who are leading inquiry have repeatedly shown us that collaborative inquiry is essential for facilitating school improvement and supporting leadership development. As an improvement strategy, inquiry does not search for the "one right answer"; but rather, it opens space for multiple strategies, processes, programs, and structures that may improve student outcomes. As a leadership development opportunity, inquiry allows teachers to focus on student achievement differently than how an individual teacher looks at student progress. Through inquiry with a collaborative group, there are opportunities to question assumptions, school structures and group processes that systematically or unintentionally have an impact on the achievement of particular groups of students (Olsen, 1999; Weissglass, 2001). A collaborative group at a school can look across classrooms and grades at outcomes and patterns in student achievement. Exploring those patterns holds great promise for meeting the goals of not just providing similar opportunities for all students, but also ensuring quality outcomes for all students, no matter their race, ethnicity, home language or economic level. Teachers are the ones who must lead these inquiry efforts and difficult conversations, as they are the ones who will be, and are, called upon to ensure that every student leaving their class has the knowledge, skills, and habits of mind to be successful in our society.

Questions for Reflection/Classroom Exercises
Stepping into being a Teacher Leader

1. Explore the various leadership roles that teachers take at your school (e.g., grade level leader, committee chairperson, etc.) and district. Talk with some of these teacher leaders about what matters most to them in their work and how they came to be in these leadership positions. Clarify your own goals. Make a list of leadership opportunities that interest you. Make a plan for steps you could take to step into leadership roles.

2. Seek out the ELL and Special Education teachers in your school. Talk together about how students get identified for these services and how they are exited from the programs. As a group, look at the gender and ethnicity information for students in these programs. When do students enter these programs and when do they leave? If the group can't easily answer these questions, collect information and explore these issues.

3. Work with other teachers at your grade level to identify achievement issues that are of the highest concern to the group. Find out what information is already collected by the school (test scores, attendance, discipline, grades) and look at that information as a group. Does that information show the same pattern that concerns the grade level teachers? Talk about the types of local information (e.g., student work) that teachers in the group might be willing to collect and bring to the group to share. Set up a schedule for meeting and sharing. Keep notes from the discussions. In the discussions, refer back to the issues that were first identified. Focus on how teachers can interrupt these patterns to ensure that all students in their classrooms achieve to high standards. Share lessons that work well with students who are struggling. Look again at data at the end of the year to see how the achievement patterns have changed.

Table 11.1
Classroom Inquiry as an Exploration of Equity

For your own students,

1. Look at the standardized test results that are available to you, and disaggregate (separate and organize) those results in several ways:
   - student ethnicity
   - home language
   - number of years at your school

2. Collect other local data:
   - grade reports
   - attendance
   - discipline records

3. Map those results into the same categories that you did the standardized test results.

4. Do you see similar patterns for any particular group of students?

5. Find a colleague and discuss your findings.

6. Begin to enlarge the circle of data that you are reviewing from your own classroom to a cohort of students across grade levels (e.g., look at their performance in second, third, and fourth grades) or a particular grade level (e.g., this year's fourth graders).

Chapter 12

Teaching Through the Arts:
A Missing Link in Bilingual and Multicultural Education

by Peter Baird

The function of art has always been to break through the crust of conventionalized and routine consciousness... Artists have always been the real purveyors of the news, for it is not the outward happening in itself which is new, but the kindling by it of emotion, perception, appreciation.

John Dewey (1946)

(T)eaching for social justice is teaching for the sake of arousing the kinds of vivid, reflective, experimental responses that might move students to come together in serious efforts to understand what social justice actually means and what it might demand. That means teaching to the end of arousing a consciousness of membership, active and participant membership in a society of unfulfilled promises --- teaching for what Paulo Freire called "conscientization", heightened social consciousness, a wide-awakeness that might make injustice unendurable.

Maxine Greene (1998)

Introduction

As we find ourselves amid yet another, and certainly deeper, economic recession – one that seems to be challenging the very existence of public education – the role of teaching through and about the arts to children and young people certainly falls squarely on the shoulders of our overburdened classroom teachers. This chapter is dedicated to you who continue to believe and teach your beliefs so that all children can receive an equitable and multicultural education.

The purpose of this chapter is twofold: first of all to show how one bilingual teacher, now a teacher educator, has used critical theory and participatory research methodology in his teaching and research journey over the past ten years; secondly, it is to offer suggestions to other teachers on how to apply this research to our children and classrooms.

The focus of my story is about teaching through the multicultural arts ----- one crucial component that is too often missing from public school programs for working class and culturally and linguistically diverse children. Teaching about, with and through the arts is not only forced into a minimal role in public school classrooms, it is often dismissed from many teacher preparation programs throughout the U.S. Surely it is not the only thing missing from our public schools, as the other authors of this book have made clear, but as John Dewey and Maxine Greene so eloquently reminds us above, the arts are essential to reawaken radical hope for social transformation.

As the previous authors have illustrated in this collection, we are in critical need of critical theory, especially now that the election of President Barack Obama has challenged decades of war economy, deportations, budget constraints and what Kris Gutierrez (2000) calls "backlash politics (p.7)". Here are three reasons why critical theory is so important to educators at this time and place:

1. *Current educational policy and practice in the U.S. are dominated not by theory, but rather by ideology* – more specifically, a neo-conservative ideology with a corporate agenda to ultimately privatize public education (People for the American Way Foundation Report, 2003). Even factual data-collection and honest analysis by hands-on teachers of what we experience is thus very important in providing students an opportunity to critically observe the world and apply it to their lives.

2. *When educators analyze the much-discussed "achievement gap" for poor and minority children, we need to be guided by "critical" questions.* Educators are more likely to take action when we seek answers for questions such as who benefits and who is hurt by policies such as No Child Left Behind (NCLB), charter schools and the accountability movement. These are complex issues, but are irrelevant without critical analysis.

3. *Teachers at all levels and of all backgrounds need to feel empowered that we can serve the needs of our students and work for social justice in our schools, communities, nation and the international community.* This means that our separate experiences and analysis are improved when they are guided by critical theory and contribute to its ongoing formation.

Just what is critical theory and how is it linked to my life as an educator? For me, it is an approach to looking at education and the world with the goal of transforming it – what Alma Flor Ada and Isabel Compoy (2004) have described so well in *Authors in the Classroom: A Transformative Education Process.* While the book itself is a guide for teachers to deepen their teaching by becoming authors of their own classroom experience, the opening chapter on Theoretical Principals is also a very useful and comprehensible summary of key insights from various disciplines and writers who have developed them, even more compacted below (Ada & Campoy, 2004, p. 10-15):

- Constructivist Theory: Human beings are beings of knowledge (Vygotsky; Freire, Ferreiro & Gomez Palacio; Smith).
- Feminist/Womanist Theory: Human beings are beings of love and caring (Gilligan; hooks; Pinkola-Éstes; Lorde).
- Aesthetics: Human beings are intrinsically drawn to beauty (Greene).
- Critical Theory: Human beings are the sole creators of social reality. As such, we are responsible for participating in its ongoing creation and improvement (Adorno & Horkheimer; Marcuse; Gramsci; Freirel Habermasl Giroux).
- Multiculturalism: The earth is diverse in its very nature. Human beings are diverse as the reality of this planet (Nieto; Takaki; Delpit).
- Anti-Bias Education: To become fully human, we must unlearn prejudice and bias and become one another's allies (Herover-Marcuse; Derman-Sparks et.al.; Derman-Sparks & Phillops; Delpit,; Lee, Menhart & Okozawa-Rey; Tatum, Reza).
- Critical Pedagogy: Throughout the world, most forms of public education promote the domestication and colonialization of the human mind in order to maintain the status quo (Freire; Freire & Macedo; Poplin & Weeres; Shor & Freire; Walsh; Wink).
- Bilingual Education: Language is one of the strongest elements in our self-definition, as well as one of the most significant elements of culture (Ada; Ada & Campoy; Baker; Brisk; Brisk & Homington; Cunnins; Fishman; Krashen; Skutnabb-Kangas; Skutnabb-Kangas, Phillipson & Rannut; Wong-Filmore).

From Elementary to College Classroom

My personal path as an educator began as a third career, following years of social activism, journalism, musicianship, and work as a journeyman printer. I was a bilingual elementary teacher in rural Galt, south of Sacramento, teaching the children of Mexican workers, with limited curriculum, but lots of high expectations. I loved to use music, plays, family literacy and other means to make my classroom come alive, but I felt isolated from the social justice movement. My fellow teachers were surprisingly conservative, except in the areas of union issues and their advocacy of bilingual education. When I heard about a doctoral program in International and Multicultural Education at the University of San Francisco, I was excited and eventually was brought along by friends like Dr. Nancy Jean Smith and her mentor, Dr. Alma Flor Ada.

Like many others before me and since, I continued teaching during the week, but joined the doctoral program on the teaching weekends – every other week. I jumped directly into a course on Participatory Research by Dr. Ada. I soon realized that this was a methodology that deeply resonated with my experience as a journalist and writer. . As Ada and Buetel wrote at USF in 1993,

> To transform the world. To amplify the voices of those who are rendered
> voiceless by the dominant society. To inscribe with them their words
> and wisdom. To provide the stage where women and men, children, the
> elderly, and the disenfranchised minorities and communities become
> the protagonists of their own life stories. These are the intentions of
> Participatory Research. (p. 53)

Moreover, I came to see that this methodology of inserting oneself into the dialogue with participants in the educational process provided me with an ideal mode for reflecting on my practice as a teacher and activist. Dr. Ada guided us through this class and many others over the three years, challenging us to become researchers and critical multicultural educators. In December of 1999, in the midst of our dissertation writing, she told us:

> You are developing a new aspect of your personality; that of a researcher.
> You have been many things in your life—social service person, teachers,
> counselors, advisors, you've been many things. Now you're adding.
> You've been researchers too, but you've been researchers without
> acknowledging to yourself that you were. (Baird, P. 1999)

What would I focus on for my dissertation research? I had so many unanswered questions from my teaching experiences, too many ideas, and did not know where to begin. I vividly remember my first doctoral retreat with Dr. Ada when I found her alone long enough to ask her what was the "best" topic of three I'd considered: parent involvement, bilingual instruction strategies, or something having to do with teaching children through music. She smiled at me and asked, "What is the one that you are most passionate about, that touches your heart?" I actually felt my heart beat in my chest as I responded "the music, of course," and it was decided. (Baird, P. 1999 Journal).

Much to my surprise, at the end of my second year of the three year IME program, I was offered a teaching position in the Bilingual/Multicultural Department at CSU Sacramento. I changed jobs and began to teach the young adults in our program just as I was entering the crucial dissertation phase of my doctoral program. The participatory research process led me to seek out significant children's musicians in the U.S. who have nurtured children over the decades with their socially-uplifting songs and teachings. I traveled to San Jose to dialogue with Suni Paz, to Chicago to meet Ella Jenkins, and to New York to spend time with Pete Seeger – asking them and six other talented practitioners my key questions about how they practice their songmaking craft. A first dialogue was shared with the participant, who often responded in writing and helped to analyze the lessons learned. One participant, the extremely busy Pete Seeger, carried the dialogue even further than I could have imagined by reading the finished manuscript and offered editorial comments and corrections throughout.

Equally important was the advising process with Dr. Ada. These sessions began in classes or in her office, but as time went on our sessions were squeezed in at the White Retreat Center in Marin County where many of Alma Flor's current and former students gathered each semester. Alma Flor drummed it into our heads at each meeting: "don't work alone; … form learning groups;… share your writing; …support each other," and I'm glad to say that we followed her advice.

Eventually the participatory research and writing was completed, resulting in four sets of "Recommendations for Action" – for parents and the wider community, public elementary and preschools, teacher education programs at colleges and universities, and children's music advocacy organizations. Two of these areas are listed below:

Recommendations for Preschool and Elementary School Teachers

1. Rethink the role of singing and the arts as being one of the main ways to reach all children – create a multicultural community, encourage peacemaking and problem-solving, teach the values of social justice and service to the community, unite the curriculum, and make school a more fun place to be for students and staff. Make it part of your school philosophy and allow it to reshape your school environment. Get rid of the ideas that only the "gifted" can sing and that music is another contest to see who is the best competitor.

2. Hire well-rounded music teachers in every school who can support a new vision of music education and singing by working closely with classroom teachers and staff to plan assemblies, school-wide group singing, community programs, and partnerships with outside artists. If there are no credentialed music teachers available who can do this, look to outside artists and song-makers, as many schools already do. Music teachers should be trainers and motivators, not roving "prep" teachers who never get to interact with the regular classroom teachers.

3. Select songs which exhibit some of the essential characteristics of teachable songs: a singable melody, good rhythm, repetitive form, humorous, balanced between specific and universal, respectful of children's intelligence, authentic, adaptable, multicultural and multilingual, familiar enough to sing, and telling a good story about real people.

4. Encourage classroom teachers to meet the needs of their students by integrating fun and meaningful songs and other art forms into their everyday teaching. This can be done through collaborations with music/singing teachers and outside song-makers, school in-service trainings, district workshops and other means. Remind teachers that children follow their example; participation is essential. Hire teachers who are excited about reaching their students through the arts.

5. Communicate to colleges, universities and credentialing institutions that new teachers, especially those teaching ethnically and linguistically diverse children, need preparation to be able to teach to the whole child, including through music and kinesthetic modalities that are addressed through song-making.

6. Provide teachers with resources to involve children in singing, including music recordings, songbooks and capable people to demonstrate their use. Include

resources that reflect the folk music traditions of the United States and the world community, which will in turn reflect enduring values of social justice.

7. Reach beyond the traditional school environment and build partnerships with a wide variety of artistic and community organizations that can enrich the lives of students and staff. Involve multicultural song-makers like those in this study to help set up short-range programs and long-range partnerships. They are the proven experts in this field and have shared just a small portion of their experience through this research.

8. Design new schools and modify the existing ones to make room for children to sing together.

9. Encourage parents and family members to share their music in school settings, as part of an overall program of having the local school meet the needs of the parents and the surrounding community.

10. Make time each week for staff and children to come together and sing for fun and social justice. It will build community, promote literacy, foster multicultural inclusion, model good pedagogy for teachers, teach social responsibility, and make everyone feel good. (Consequently, it will probably raise test scores too.)

Recommendations for Teacher Educators at Colleges and Universities:

1. Advocate and incorporate the actions listed above into your education programs for new and experienced teachers. Support those elementary and preschool teachers who are already doing transformative song-making and ask them to help you.

2. Retool the whole idea of music and arts education along the lines suggested by the participants, kicking out the competitive model of music in favor of one that fosters participation, creativity, imagination and – here's the most important one – love of singing.

3. Use transformative song-making as a way to raise consciousness of new and returning teachers to the central role of social justice in public education. Have students read John Dewey, Maxine Greene, Paulo Freire, Alma Flor Ada, Bonnie Lockhart and Pete Seeger.

4. Bring music and, in particular, singing back to your theory and methods courses as one of the most pleasurable and effective means of teaching children language, social studies, math, science and music. Pre-service teachers need to have singing and other artistic experiences themselves to become effective teachers, especially if they were denied it in their early years. This is essential for classroom teachers at the elementary level and doubly true for music teachers.

5. Prepare teachers of immigrant children and culturally and linguistically diverse students to use songs, poetry, and chants as Total Physical Response activities – all research-proven techniques of second language acquisition. English learner students are now the majority in California schools, and other states are facing similar challenges.

6. Draw upon children's musicians and other community artists to come in as visiting lecturers, guest artists and part-time faculty to share their experiences with pre-service teachers, especially if current faculty are not prepared to teach about transformative song-making. This may involve collaborating with the local arts community and organization such as the Children's Music Network. Some of the most talented song-makers may be classroom and music teachers from nearby public schools, who constitute another rich resource for higher education. (Baird, P. 2001. p. 200-205)

The other recommendations from the study not included here are complementary – parents can foster the arts at home with their children and actively engage their local schools, and arts organizations can offer their talents and services to public schools, especially those who serve children in poor communities. The same, of course, can and should be said for the other visual and performing arts that are equally missing from many of our public schools: the visual, dramatic and dance/movement arts.

Passing it On

As I finished my research and began teaching at CSU Sacramento, I wondered if I was following my own recommendations. It certainly didn't feel like it, even when I toted my guitar to all my classes and got my students singing about the subjects and causes we were learning about. The 1970 Ryan Act in California had eliminated the art-course requirements for elementary teachers. As a result, few credential programs, including my own, had any arts-related methods courses. Happily, in 2001 the California Commission on Teacher Credentialing reversed an old error and added a requirement for accreditation to include "some training in the teaching of visual and performing arts" (California Alliance for Arts Education, 2008). Before the new requirement took effect in 2004, my department chair asked me to design the class for our multiple-subject teacher candidates. I gladly accepted the challenge to begin to actualize my research findings.

The class, EDBM 320, is titled "Curriculum and Instruction for Elementary Bilingual/Multicultural Classrooms: Teaching Through the Visual and Performing Arts," – for short, it's know as the VAPA class. The course goals are based on the California Department of Education Standards for Arts in the Classroom (2008). The VAPA class has been a delightful journey of discovery. After teaching about VAPA standards and how they can be multicultural and transformative in nature, I model what I know best (participatory singing) and bring in outside teacher/artist experts to model other disciplines and applications for music, dance/movement, visual arts and drama. Then they choose one discipline group to investigate throughout the semester and present their findings as "expert groups." Throughout the process we come to learn about each other as singers, dancers, visual artists, and theatrical performers, then how we can model and facilitate these kinds of learning experiences in our classrooms. Often we have special guest presenters, such as local teachers who have been trained in Project G.L.A.D. (Guided Language Acquisition Design) – a very effective and popular model that incorporates many visual and performing arts strategies into standards-based education. As their website describes, "GLAD is a model of professional development in the area of language acquisition and literacy. The strategies and model promote English language acquisition, academic achievement, and cross-cultural skills (Project G.L.A.D. 2009).

At the end of the class each VAPA student turns in several lesson plans describing how they have taught literacy, math, science, social studies and other subjects using the multicultural arts, including a critical reflection on how it impacted the learning experience. They also produce and share their own autobiographical book focused on introducing themselves to their future students, inspired by *Authors in the Classroom* (Ada & Campoy 2004). Finally, each student produces an Action Plan for how he or she will teach through the arts in their own classrooms. The following, for example, is a compelling and creative action plan by Donya Harding, a Spring 2008 graduate of the BMED Multiple Subject program:

Even in the midst of an Open Court/Saxon Math juggernaut or any other scripted program that teachers must teach because of No Child Left Behind, teachers can still infuse the arts to make these curricula more interesting, more comprehensible and more culturally relevant.

I will encourage students to draw, write, sing and dance. I will give them the options to use these artistic abilities in lieu of simply reading an oral report. In the past, I have had preschoolers re-enact slave escapes via the Underground Railroad; I have written a rap song to help English Learners remember the importance of nutrition; and I have exposed my students to a variety of visual arts, dance and music. My challenge is to continue to do so regardless of pressures to teach to the tests and raise test scores. My philosophy is "If you teach a child to memorize, they will probably forget; but if you teach a child to think, they will learn to succeed." (Action Plan, unpublished, 2008)

The connections between understanding critical theory, putting it into practice with multicultural arts in the classroom, and then being able to communicate the experience to others is what Paulo Freire (1972) called "praxis." I am reminded that while we seem to stand alone, we are, in fact, standing on the shoulders of those who have come before us. The coauthors and I are surely standing on the capable shoulders of Alma Flor Ada and all those who have inspired and influenced her.

As for the importance of singing and experiencing the arts with young people as we go about the work of transforming our communities, I certainly agree with children's musician Bonnie Lockhart (1998) that "it will take more than songs to bring equity to education … But surrounding ourselves with music, the music we make with young children, I know we'll find what we need for the long haul (p. 124)."

Reflection Questions:

1. What are some of the critical questions that you and your colleagues are asking about education? Who is being hurt the most by the current budget cuts, and why?

2. Who has influenced your formation as an educator? How have you influenced others?

3. How are the arts included, or excluded, from your school or teacher credential program? Which of the recommendations for action in this chapter do you think are most applicable to your school or program? How do you teach your students with, through and about the multicultural arts?

4. Do you have skills in the visual and performing arts that you share with your students? Are there other teachers, parents and friends who you could learn from, or invite to your classroom?

5. Is there a multicultural arts team at your school or program? Who do you know with passion and skills in this area? How would you go about setting one up? Who are the parents and community resources that could be called upon?

REFERENCES

Forward

Freire, P. (1997). Pedagogy of hope: Reliving pedagogy of the oppressed. New New York: Continuum

Chapter 1: Going Beyond Heroes and Holidays

Ada, A.F. (1997). Language and transformative education: Reader: *Linguistic human rights and education.* San Francisco: University of San Francisco.

Ada, A. F. (2003). *A magical encounter: Latino children's literature in the classroom.* Boston: Pearson Education.

Ada, A.F., Campoy, F. I. (2000). *Readings on anti-bias education curriculum: A theoretical introduction.* San Francisco: University of San Francisco.

Banks, J. (1994). *An introduction to multicultural education.* Boston: Allyn and Bacon

Banks, J. (2001). *Cultural diversity and education: Foundation, curriculum, and teaching,* 4ed. Boston: Allyn and Bacon.

Darder, A., Torres, R.D., & Gutierrez, H. (1997). *Latinos and education: A critical reader.* New York: Routledge.

Gay, G. (2002). Preparing for culturally responsive teaching. *Journal of Teacher Education,* 53, (2): 106-116.

Ladson-Billings, G. (1994). *The dreamkeepers: Successful teachers of African American children.* San Francisco: Jossey Bass.

Macedo, D. (2006). *Literacies of power: What Americans are not allowed to know.* Boulder, Co: Westview Press.

Neophytos Richardson, A. (2001). Teaching critical writing to secondary students: Speaking our worlds. In Ramirez, L & Gallardo, O. (Eds.), *Portraits of teachers in multicultural settings: A critical literacy approach.* (pp. 105-121) Boston: Allyn & Bacon.

Nieto, S. (2002). *Language, culture, and teaching: Critical perspectives for a new century.* Mahwah, N.J.: Lawrence Erlbaum Associates.

Noddings, N. (2003). *Caring: A feminine approach to ethics and moral education,* 2nd ed. Berkeley: University of California Press.

Olson. L. & Jaramillo, A. (1999). *Turning the tides of exclusion: A guide for educators and advocates for Immigrant students.* Oakland: California Tomorrow.

Pang, V. (2005). *Multicultural education: A caring-centered, reflective approach,* 2nd ed. Boston, MA: McGraw Hill.

Ramirez, L. Gallardo, O. (Eds.). (2001). *Portraits of teachers in multicultural settings: A critical literacy approach.* Boston: Allyn and Bacon.

Valenzuela, A. (1999). *Subtractive schooling.* Albany: State University of New York Press

Villegas, A., & Lucas, T., (2002). Preparing culturally responsive teachers: Rethinking the curriculum. *Journal of Teacher Education,* 53: 20-32.

Wallerstein, N., Auerback, E. (2004). Problem- Posing at Work: Popular educator's guide. Alberta: Grassroots Press.

Wink, J. (2004). *Critical pedagogy: Notes from the real world.* Boston: Allyn & Bacon

Wlodlkowski, R., Ginsberg, M. (1995). *Diversity & motivation: Culturally responsive teaching.* NY: Jossey-Bass.

Chapter 2: Transforming Pancho Villa

Baruth, R. (2004). Those who dare, teach: Living a pedagogy for social justice. In J. O'Donnell, M., Pruyn, R. & Chavez Chavez (eds). *Social justice in these times.* (pp. 33-53). Connecticut: Information Age Publishing.

Combs, M. (1996). Emerging readers and writers in L. Dixon-Krauss, (ed.) *Vygotsky in the classroom: Mediated literacy instruction and assessment.* (pp. 25-41). New York: Longman Publishers.

Freire, P. (1996). *Pedagogy of the oppressed.* (Myra Bergman Ramos, Trans.) (Original work published 1970). New York: Continuum Publishing.

Hernández, A. (2003). Making content accessible for English language learners. In G. Garcia, (ed.) *English learners: Reaching the highest level of English literacy.* (pp. 125-149). International Reading Association.

Macedo, D. (2006) *Literacies of power: What Americans are not allowed to know.* Boulder, CO: Westview Press.

Thomas, W.P., & Collier V.P. (2001) A National Study of School Effectiveness for Language Minority Students Long-term Academic Achievement. Center for Research on Education, Diversity & Excellence (CREDE), a National research center funded by the Office of Educational Research and Improvement (OERI) of the U.S. Department of Education.

Chapter 3: Unlearning Racism

Calhoun, E.F. (1994). How to use Action Research in the Self-Renewing School Alexandria, VA: ASCD Publications.

Freire, P. (1993). *Pedagogy of the oppressed.* New York: The Continuum Publishing Company.

Henze, R. C. et al. (2002). *Leading for diversity: How school leaders promote positive interethnic relations.* California: Corwin Press, Inc.

Lambert, L. (1998). *Building Leadership Capacity in Schools.* Alexandria, VA: ASCD Publications

Perez, P. (2008). *Educators as adult learners creating sustainable community development through solicitude and care for the other: Critical inquiry in Northern California and North East Thailand.* Unpublished doctoral dissertation, University of San Francisco.

Ramírez, L. & Gallardo, O. (2001). *Portraits of teachers in multicultural settings: A critical literacy approach.* Boston, MA: Allyn & Bacon.

B.D, (1999). *Why are all the Black kids sitting together in the cafeteria? And other conversations about race.* New York: Basic Books.

Chapter 4: Collaboration and Community Transformed Center Stage

Freire, P. (2000). *Pedagogy of the oppressed.* New York: Continuum Publishing Company.

Gibbs, J. & Huang, L. (2001). *Children of color: psychological interventions with culturally diverse youth.* San Francisco, CA: Jossey-Bass Publishers.

Goldman, D. (1995). *Emotional intelligence.* New York, NY: Bantam Books.

Loewen, J. (1995). *Lies my teacher told me.* New York, NY: Simon & Schuster.

Youth in Focus. Davis High School. Davis, CA. May 17, 2004. Community Presentation: Expectations of student performance at Davis High School: Are they different by the race/ethnicity of the student? Findings from a student-led research project.

Zinn, H. (1999). *A people's history of the United States*. New York, NY: Harper Collins Publishers.

Chapter 5: Honoring And Sustaining Heritage Languages

*Adesope, Lavin, Thompson, and Ungerleider (2010), A Systematic Review and Meta-analysis of the Cognitive Correlates of Bilingualism, *Review of Educational Research*, Vol.80, and No.2. Pp 207-245

*http://www.CaliforniansTogether.org. – *Seal of Biliteracy*: proposal, sample CSBA policy, and administrative regulations.

*Cummins, James (1989). Empowering minority students: A framework for intervention, *Harvard Education Review*, 56 (1), 13-18.

Banks, James, A (2001). *Cultural Diversity and Education: Foundations, Curriculum, and Teaching,* fourth edition. Allyn & Bacon.

Bialystok, E., & Majumder, S (1998) the relationship between bilingualism and the development of cognitive processes in problem solving. *Applied Psycholinguistics* 19, 69-85.

Bialystok, E., Craik, F.I. M., Grady, C., Chau, W., Ishii, R., Gunji, A., & Pantev, C (2005). Effect of bilingualism on cognitive control in the Simon task: Evidence from MEG. *NeuroImage*, 24, 40-49.

* Bialystok, E., Craik, F.I.M., & Luk, G (2008). cognitive control and lexical access in younger and older bilinguals. *Journal of Experimental Psychology: Learning, Memory and Cognition,* 34, 859-873.

*Gutierrez-Clellen, V. F., Calderon, J., & Weismer, S. E. (2004). Verbal working memory in bilingual children. *Journal of Speech, Language and Hearing Research*, 47, 863-876.

*Nieto, S., & Bode, P., (2008). *Affirming Diversity: The sociopolitical context of multicultural education*, Fifth Edition, p 427, 428, 429.

Peal, E., & Lambert, W.E. (1962). The relation of bilingualism to intelligence. *Psychological Monographs*, 76, 1-23.

*Olsen, L. & Jaramillo, A. (1999), *Turning the tides of exclusion*: *A guide for educators and advocates for immigrant students*. California Tomorrow: Oakland, p 213

Olsen, L. (2010). *Reparable Harm: Fulfilling the Unkept Promise of Educational Opportunity for California's Long Term English Learners*. http://www. CaliforniansTogether.org/reports/

*Skutnabb-Kangas, T., Philipson, R. (Ed) & Rannut, M. (1994), *Linguistic Human Rights*: *Overcoming linguistic discrimination*. Mounton de Gruyter.

Chapter 6: Transformative Education in Action

Banks, J. (1991). *Teaching strategies for ethnic studies*. Boston, MA: Allyn & Bacon.

Center for Korean Studies, University of California, Los Angeles Available: http://www.isop.ucla.edu/korea/

Center for Korean Studies, University of Hawaii Available: http://www2.hawaii.edu/korea

Chan, S. (1990). Mary Paik Lee: A pioneer Korean woman in America. In *Quiet odyssey*. (2nd ed.). University of Washington Press.

Chan, S. (1998). Families with Asian roots. In E. W. Lynch & M. J. Hanson (Eds.), *Developing cross-cultural competence: A guide for working with young children and their families* (2nd ed.), 251-354, Baltimore: Paul H. Brookes.

Cho, E. (1998). *The role of communication in providing effective special education services for Korean-American children with specific learning disabilities: A participatory study*. Doctoral Dissertation: University of San Francisco.

Cho, E. (1993). *Korean American parents' attitudes toward their children or youth with disabilities and their education in the United States*. Master of Arts Thesis: California State University, Sacramento.

Collier, C., Hoover, J.J. (1987). *Cognitive learning strategies for minority handicapped students*. Lindale, TX: Hamilton Publications.

Gudykunst, W.B., Matsumoto, Y., Ting-Toomey, S., Nishida, T., Kim, K., & Heyman, S. (1996). *The influence of cultural construal and individual values on communication styles across cultures, human communication individualism-collectivism*. *Self Research, 22* (4), 510-543. *Handbook for teaching Korean-American students* (1992).

Harry, B., Grenot-Scheyer, M., Smith-Lewis, M., Park, H.S., Xin, F., & Schwartz, I. (1994). *Developing culturally inclusive services for individuals with severe disabilities.*

Hernandez, H. (1989). *Special/Gifted education: Multicultural connections. Multicultural education: A teacher's guide to content and process.* 107-138. New York, Macmillan Publishing Company

Hur, S. V., & Hur, B. S. (1999). *Culture shock! Korea.* Portland, OR: Graphic Arts Center Publishing Co.

Hurh, W. & M. Kim, K. C. (1984). *Korean immigrants in North America: Structural analysis of ethnic confinement and adhesive adaptation.* Madison: Fairleigh Dickinson University Press.

Individuals with Disabilities Education Act (1997)

Kagitcibasi, C. (1992). Human behavior in global perspective: An introduction to cross-cultural psychology. *Journal of Cross-Cultural Psychology*, 23 (1), 116-120.

Kalyanpur, M., Harry, B. (1999). *Culture in special education: Building reciprocal family-professional relationships.* Baltimore: Paul H. Brookes.

Kalyanpur, M., Rao (1991). Empowering low-income Black families of handicapped children. *American Journal of Orthopsychiatry, 61*, 523-532.

Katsiyannis, A. Conderman, G. (1994). Section 504 Policies and Procedures-An established necessity. *Remedial and Special Education, 15*, 311-318.

Kim, I. (1981). *New urban immigrants: The Korean community in New York.* Princeton, NJ: Princeton University Press.

Kim-Rupnow, W.S. (2001). An introduction to Korean culture for rehabilitation service providers. A monograph written as part of an eleven-volume monograph series. *The rehabilitation provider's guide to cultures of the foreign-born.* Center for International Rehabilitation Research Information and Exchange (CIRRIE), New York, Buffalo: University of New York at Buffalo.

Korea Institute of Harvard University Available: http://www.fas.harvard.edu/~korea/index_home.html

Lehrer, B. Stotsky, S. (1996). *The immigrant experience: The Korean Americans.* New York: Chelsea House Publishers.

Min, P. G. (1984c). From white-collar occupations to small business: Korean immigrants' occupational adjustment." *Sociological Quarterly, 25*:333-352.

186

Mindel, C. H., Habenstein, R.W. Roosevelt Wright, Jr. (1988). The Korean American family. *Ethnic families in America.* (3 ed.), (pp. 199-229). Prentice-Hall, Inc.

National Center for the Dissemination of Disability Research Southwest Educational Development Laboratory (NCDDR) (1999). Disability, diversity, and dissemination: A review of the literature on topics related to increasing the utilization of rehabilitation research outcomes among diverse consumer groups. Available: http://www.ncddr.org/du/products/dddreview/index.html

National Research Council. (2002). *Minority students in special and gifted education.* Washington, D.C.: National Research Press.

No Child Left Behind Act (2002).

Park, J., Turnbull, A. P., Park, H. (2001). Quality of partnerships in service provision for Korean American parents of children with disabilities: A qualitative inquiry, *JASH.* 26(3), 158-170.

Randall-David, E. (1989). *Strategies for working with culturally diverse communities and clients.* Rocksville, MD: The Association for the Care of Children's Health.

Rehabilitation Research Information and Exchange (CIRRIE). Available: http://cirrie. buffalo.edu/monographs/korea.pdfs

The Korean Studies Program at the University of Washington Available:http://jsis.artsci. washington.edu/programs/korea/korea.html

The U.S. Census Bureau: Census 2000 Special Reports (December, 2004), U.S. Department of Commerce Economics and Statistics Administration, U.S. CENSUS BUREAU CENSR-17

Turnbull, A. P., & Turnbull, H. R., (2001). *Families, professionals, and exceptionality: Collaborating for empowerment* (4th ed.). Upper Saddle River, NJ: Merrill/ Prentice-Hall.

U.S. Census Bureau (May, 2001). Profiles of general demographic characteristics 2000 Retrieved from http://www.census.gov/prod/cen2000/doc/ProfilesTD.pdfU.S. Census Bureau (January 13, 2000). Projections of the resident population by race, Hispanic origin, and nativity: Middle Series, 2050 to 2070. Retrieved from http:// www.census.gov/population/projections/nation/summary/np-t5-g.pdf

U.S. Department of Labor, Office of Disability Employment Policy (November 20, 2002). Disability and Cultural Diversity. Available: http://www.dol.gov/odep/ pubs/ek98/disabili.htm

Chapter 7: Empowered Parents Transform a School District

Baker, C. (1997). *Foundations of bilingual education and bilingualism*. 2nd ed. Bristol, PA: Multilingual Matters Ltd. California Department of Education. (1998). Title 5, California Code of Regulation. English language education for immigrant children.

California Education Code: Education Code Section 305, (1999) Sacramento, CA. California Department of Education.

Comité Pro Educación de nuestra comunidad. October 16, 1998. Violation of Law: Education Code 300-340 and Title 5, California Code Regulation, Division 1, Chapter 11, Sections 113000 Through 11305. Complaint registered January 21, 1999.

Crawford, J. (2000). The Proposition 227 Campaign: A post mortem. *At war with diversity: U.S. language policy in an age of anxiety.* (pp. 104-137). Clevedon: Multilingual Matters Ltd.

Cummins, J. (1996). *Negotiating identities: Education for empowerment in a diverse society.* Ontario: California Association of Bilingual Education.

Delgado-Gaitan, C. (1991). Involving parents in the schools: A process of empowerment. In G. Maez (Ed.), *Compendium of research on Bilingual Education* (pp.169-191). Washington D C.: George Washington University.

Echevarria, J., Vogt, M. E., & Short, D. J., (2004). *Making content comprehensible for English learners: The SIOP model.* Boston: Pearson Education.

Gold, N. (1997). Teachers for LEP students: Demand, supply and shortage. Sacramento, CA: California Department of Education, Complaints Management and Bilingual Compliance Unit.

Krashen, S., Crawford, J., & Kim, H., (1998). Bias in polls on Bilingual Education: A demonstration. *Bilingual Research Journal,* Winter 1997, 21(1).

Ramirez, J.D., Yuen, S.D., & Ramey, D.R. (1991) *Final report: Longitudinal study of structured immersion strategy, early-exit, and late-exit transitional bilingual education programs for language-minority children. Executive Summary.* San Mateo, CA: Aguirre International.

Tyler, T. (1998, November 21). Parents to fight Pittsburg's bilingual plan. *Ledger Dispatch.*

Lindholm-Leary, K.J. (2001). *Dual language education.* Clevedon Hall: Multilingual Matters LTD.

Chapter 8: Teacher Education Students Share Their Voices

Ada, A. F. & Campoy, F. I., (2004*). Authors in the classroom: A transformative education process.* New York: Pearson, Allyn & Bacon.

Hayes, C. W., Bahruth, R. & Kessler, C. (1998). *Literacy con cariño.* Portsmouth, NH: Heinemann.

Yagelski, R. P. (2000). *Literacy matters: Writing and reading the social self.* New York: Teachers College Press.

Chapter 9: Preparing Pre-Service Spanish Bilingual Teachers to Develop a Vision for Transformative Education

Arce, J., Luna, D., Borjian, A., and Conrad, M. (2006). No Child Left Behind: Who Wins, Who Loses? *Social Justice Journal.* 32 (3), 56-71.

Bigelow, B. (2006). *The line between us.* WI: Rethinking Schools.

Cummins, J. (1996). *Negotiating identities: Education for empowerment in a diverse society.* Los Angeles, CA: California Association for Bilingual Education.

Cummins, J. (2008). Rights and responsibilities of educators of bilingual/bicultural children. In Diaz Soto, L. (Ed.). *Making a difference in the lives of bilingual/bicultural children.* (4th. ed.). NY: Peter Lang.

Darder, A. (1991). *Culture and power in the classroom: A critical foundation for Bilingual Education.* Westport, CT: Bergin & Garvey.

Darder, A. (1995). Buscando America: The contributions of critical Latino educators to the academic development and empowerment of Latino students in the U.S. In Sleeter, C. & McLaren, P. (Eds.). *Multicultural education, critical pedagogy, and the politics of difference.* NY: State University of New York Press.

Darder, A., Torres, R.D. & Gutiérrez, H. (Eds.). (1997*). Latinos and education: A critical reader.* NY: Routledge.

Darder, A., Baltodano, M.P., & Torres, R.D. (Eds.). (2009). *The critical pedagogy reader.* (2nd.ed.). NY: Routledge.

Freire, P. (2004). *Pedagogy of the oppressed.* (30th. ed.). (Myra Bergman Ramos, Trans.). (Original work published 1970). NY: Continuum.

Garcia, E. E. (2001). *Hispanic in the United States Education: Raices y Alas.* NY: Rowman & Littlefield.

Giroux, H.A. (1981). *Ideology, culture, and the process of schooling.* PA: Temple University Press.

Giroux, H.A. (1983). *Theory and resistance in education: A pedagogy for the opposition.* NY: Bergin & Garvey.

Giroux, H.A. (1988). *Schooling and the struggle for public life: A critical pedagogy in modern age.* MN: University of Minnesota Press.

Hoare, Q., & Smith, G.N. (Eds. and trans.) (1997). *Prison notebooks of Antonio Gramsci.* NY: International. (Original work published 1971).

hooks, b. (1994). *Teaching to transgress: Education as the practice of freedom.* NY: Routledge.

hooks, b. (2000). *Where we stand: Class matters.* NY: Routledge. McLaren, P. (2003). *Life in schools.* (4th. ed.). NY: Allyn & Bacon.

Nieto, S. (2003). *What keeps teachers going.* NY: Teachers College Press.

Nieto, S. (2009). Bringing bilingual education out of the basement and other imperatives for teacher education. In Darder, A., Baltodano, M.P., & Torres, R.D. (Eds.). (2009).*The critical pedagogy reader* (pp. 469-482) (2nd ed.). NY: Routledge.

Ovando, C.J. & McLaren, P. (2000). *Politics of multiculturalism and bilingual education: Students and teachers caught in the crossfire.* NY: McGraw-Hill Higher Education.

Park, P. (1993). What is participatory research? A theoretical and methodological perspective. In Park, P., Brydon-Miller, M., Hall, B., & Jackson, T. (Eds.), *Voices of change:Participatory research in the United States and Canada* (pp.1-19). Westport, CT: Bergin & Garvey.

Reyes, M de la L., Halcón, J. (Eds.). (2000). *The Best for our children: Critical perspectives on literacy for Latino students.* NY: Teachers College Press.

Sleeter, C. & McLaren, P. (Eds.). (1995*). Multicultural education, critical pedagogy, and the politics of difference.* NY: State University of New York Press.

Shor, I. (Ed.). (1987). *Freire for the classroom: A sourcebook for liberatory teaching.* Portsmouth, NH: Heinemann.

Santa Ana, O. (Ed.) (2004) Tongue-Tied: The lives of multilingual children in Public Education. New York: Rowman & Littlefield.

Chapter 10: The Role of Inquiry in Teacher Leadership

Parks. S. (1999). Reducing the effect of racism in schools: *Educational Leadership, 58,* (2) 14-18.

Pollack, M. (2001). How the question we ask most about race in education is the very question we most suppress. *Educational Researcher, 30,* (9), 2-12.

Rolón, C. (2003). Educating Latino students. *Educational Leadership, 64,* (4), 40-43.

Tatum, A. (2002) Breaking down barriers that disenfranchise African-American adolescent readers in low-level tracks. *Journal of Adolescent & Adult Literacy, 44,* (1), pp. 52-63.

Facilitation and Group Processes:

Doyle, M. & Straus, D. (1976). *How to make meetings work: The new interaction method.* New York: Jove Books.

Garmston, R. & Wellman, B. (1999). *The adaptive school: A sourcebook for developing collaborative groups.* Norwood, MA: Christopher-Gordon Publishers.

Hunter, D., Bailey, B., & Taylor, B. (1995). *The art of facilitation: How to create group synergy.* Cambridge, MA: Da Capo Press.

Hunter, D., Bailey, B., & Taylor, B. (1995). *The Zen of groups: The handbook for people meeting with a purpose.* Cambridge, MA: Fisher Books.

Patterson, K., Grenny, J., McMillan, R., & Switzer, A. (2002). *Crucial conversations: Tools for talking when stakes are high.* McGraw-Hill.

Strauss, D. (2002). *How to make collaboration work: Powerful ways to build consensus, solve problems, and make decisions.* San Francisco: Berrett-Koehler Publishers.

Supporting and Facilitating Change:

Goldenberg, C., (2004). *Successful school change: Creating settings to improve teaching and learning.* New York: Teachers College Press.

Lambert, L. (1998). *Building leadership capacity in schools.* Alexandria, VA: Association for Supervision and Curriculum Development.

Lambert L. (2002). A framework for shared leadership. *Educational Leadership, 59,* (8), 37-42.

Lambert, L. (2003). *Leadership capacity for lasting school improvement.* Alexandria, VA: Association for Supervision and Curriculum Development.

Murphy, C.U. & Lick, D.W. (2001). *Whole-faculty study groups: Creating student-based professional development*. (2nd ed.). Thousand Oaks, CA: Corwin Press.

Chapter 11: Teaching for Voice

Delgado, R. (1995). Legal storytelling: Storytelling for oppositionists and others: A plea for narrative. In R. Delgado (Ed.), *Critical race theory: The cutting edge*. Philadelphia: Temple University Press.

Delgado, R., and Stefancic, J. (2001). *Critical race theory: An introduction*. New York University Press;

Gay, G. (1994). *At the essence of learning: Multicultural Education*. Lafayette, Ind: Kappa Delta Phi.

Gay, G. (2000). Culturally responsive teaching: Theory, research, and practice. New York: Teachers College Press.

Jennings, J. & Rentner, D. S. (2006). *Closing the achievement gap*. National Urban League.

Knaus, C. (2007) *Race, racism, and multiraciality in American education*. Bethesda LLC: Academica Press.

Delgado, R. (Ed.) (1995?). *Critical race theory: The cutting edge*. Philadelphia: Temple University Press.

Fisher, M.R. (2007). Writing in rhythm: Spoken word poetry in urban classrooms. Teachers College Press: New York.

Freire, P. (1970). *Education for critical consciousness*. New York: Continuum.

Giroux, H. (2001). *Theory and resistance in education: Towards a pedagogy for the opposition*. Conneticut: Bergin & Garvey.

Darling-Hammond, L., & Berry, B. (2006, November.). Highly qualified teachers for all. *Educational Leadership, 64*(3), 14-20.

Ladson-Billings, G. (1999). Just what is critical race theory and what's it doing in a *nice* field like education? In L. Parker, D. Deyhele, S. Villenas (Eds.) *Race is...race isn't: Critical race theory and qualitative studies in education,* 7-30. Boulder, CO: Westview Press.

Lipsitz, G. (1998). *The possessive investment in whiteness: How white people profit from identity politics*. Philadelphia, PA: Temple University Press.

Lynch, M. (2006). *Still segregated, still unequal: Analyzing the impact of No Child Left Behind on African American students.*

Macedo, D. & Bartolome, L. (1991). Dancing with bigotry. New York: St. Martins Press.

Noddings, N. (1984). *Caring: A Feminine approach to ethics and moral education.* Berkeley: University of California Press.

Oakes, J. (2005). *Keeping track: How schools structure inequality, 2nd ed.* New Haven, CT: Yale University Press

Palmer, P. (1998). *The courage to teach: Exploring the inner landscape of a teacher's life.* Jossey-Bass.

Parker, L., Deyhele, D. & Villenas S. (Eds.) *Race is...race isn't: Critical race theory and qualitative studies in education,* 7-30. Boulder, CO: Westview Press.

National Urban League. (2007). *The state of Black America.* Washington, D.C.:

Rayburn, K. (2007, September 25). Police vow complete probe of officer shooting. *Oakland Tribune.*

Swartz, E. (1992). Emancipatory narratives: Rewriting the master script in the school curriculum. *Journal of Negro Education, 61*, p. 341

Chapter 12: Teaching Through the Arts

Ada, A.F. & Buetel, C.M. (1993), *Participatory research as a dialogue for social action.* San Francisco, CA: Alma Flor Ada and Constance M. Buetel.

Ada, A.F. & Campoy, I. (2004). *Authors in the Classroom: A Transforative Education Process.* Pearson, Allison & Bacon.

Baird, P. (1999). *Journal,* unpublished.

Baird, P. (2001) *Children's Song-Makers as Messengers of Hope: Participatory Research With Implications for Teacher Educators.* UMI Number 3012660, Ann Arbor, Michigan:UMI Dissertation Services.

Baird, P. (2008) EDBM 320 Syllabus, *Curriculum & Instruction for ElementaryBilingual/ Multicultural Classrooms:Teaching Thru the Visual and Performing Arts*

California Alliance for Arts Education; Historical Context (2009) http://www.artsed411. org/educate/context.aspx

California Department of Education. (2008). *Visual and Performing Arts Content Standards for California Public Schools: Dance, Music, Theatre, Visual Arts. http://www.arts.ucla.edu/artsbridge/wp-content/themes/capoeira/pdfs/ visperfmarts-stnd-comp_1.pdf*

Dewey, J. (1946). *The public and its problems.* Chicago: Gateway Books.

Freire, P. (1972). *Pedagogy of the Oppressed*, London: Penguin.

Freire, P., & Macedo, D. (1998) Foreword. In C. Hayes, R. Baruth, & C. Kessler (Eds.) Literacy con carino. (rev.ed) Portsmouth, NH: Heinemann

Harding, Donja, (2008). "VAPA Action Plan", unpublished credential assignment, CSU Sacramento.

Lockhart, B. (1998). *"For tomorrows that sing": Relating multicultural music to anti-bias practice.* Unpublished master's thesis, Pacific Oaks College, Pasadena, CA.

People For the American Way Foundation Report (2003). *Voucher Veneer: The Deeper Agenda to Privatize Public Education.* Washington DC: People For the American Way Foundation, pfaw@pfaw.org.